Behavior Change & Public Health in the **DEVELOPING WORLD**

D0107412

John P. Elder

Behavioral Medicine & Health Psychology **4**

Sage Publications, Inc.
International Educational and Professional Publisher
Thousand Oaks ▪ London ▪ New Delhi

Copyright © 2001 by Sage Publications, Inc.

All rights reserved. No part of this book may be reproduced or utilized in any form or by any means, electronic or mechanical, including photocopying, recording, or by any information storage and retrieval system, without permission in writing from the publisher.

For information:

Sage Publications, Inc.
2455 Teller Road
Thousand Oaks, California 91320
E-mail: order@sagepub.com

Sage Publications Ltd.
6 Bonhill Street
London EC2A 4PU
United Kingdom

Sage Publications India Pvt. Ltd.
M-32 Market
Greater Kailash I
New Delhi 110 048 India

Printed in the United States of America

Library of Congress Cataloging-in-Publication Data

Elder, John P.
   Behavior change and public health in the developing world / by John P. Elder.
      p. cm. — (Behavioral medicine and health psychology)
   Includes bibliographical references and index.
   ISBN 0-7619-1778-0 (c: acid-free paper)
   ISBN 0-7619-1779-9 (p: acid-free paper)
   1. Public health—Developing countries—Psychological aspects. 2. Medicine, Preventive—Developing countries. 3. Health behavior—Developing countries. 4. Health psychology—Developing countries. I. Title. II. Behavioral medicine and health psychology (2000)
   RA441.5 .E43 2000
   614.4′4—dc21   00-009852

01   02   03   04   05   06   10   9   8   7   6   5   4   3   2   1

Acquiring Editor:	Jim Brace-Thompson
Editorial Assistant:	Anna Howland
Production Editor:	Nevair Kabakian
Editorial Assistant:	Cindy Bear
Typesetter:	Barbara Burkholder
Indexer:	Molly Hall

Contents

*To Connie Nelson Elder, for her feedback,
reinforcement, and international perspective.*

Series Editor's Introduction

Behavior Change and Public Health in the Developing World is the fourth volume in this book series. In an extremely engaging manner, Professor John Elder accomplishes two goals. First, he introduces the reader to the discipline of public health and describes the relationship between behavioral risk factors and disease. Second, he provides a powerful and moving description of how desperately the science of behavioral science is needed worldwide to fight disease and to promote health. Examples of the topics covered include tobacco use, nutrition, infectious diseases, home hygiene, family planning, breast-feeding, respiratory infections, and vaccination.

As health psychology and behavioral medicine have matured as scientific disciplines, there has been a growing awareness in the United States and other developed countries that research findings and implications need to be appropriately disseminated, not only in academic journals to fellow professionals, but also in readily accessible ways to health policy makers and to the general public. Dr. Elder shows how this awareness needs to be taken to the global level and describes the implementation of behavioral change programs in the arena of international health.

It is certainly true that disease exists in developed countries, and that a variety of behaviors are contributory factors. Nevertheless, stark contrasts can be made between developed and developing countries. Consider three examples. First, although generalizations are by definition never completely accurate, it is often the case that disease related to nutritional factors in developed countries is a consequence of "too much," whereas it is a consequence of "too little" in many developing regions of the world. About 33% of American adults are obese: In contrast, 20% of the world's population does not receive an adequate daily caloric intake. Second, developing countries have different patterns of mortality than developed countries. For example, children in the poorest countries of Africa and Asia are 20 times more likely to die by their 5th birthday than children born in the United States. Third, although AIDS is clearly a serious health problem in developed countries, its magnitude is even greater, and its threat less acknowledged by local authorities, in other regions of the world. AIDS continues to devastate Africa, and it is spreading rapidly in Asia. Behavior-change programs and public health strategies are extremely important tools in the worldwide fight against AIDS.

Dr. Elder is professor of public health in the Graduate School of Public Health at San Diego State University. My thanks are extended to him for writing a most illuminating testimony to the power of, and the critical need for, behavior-change and public health approaches in the developing countries of our world. I have no doubt that you will find his book compelling, compassionate, and extremely instructive.

—J. Rick Turner
Chapel Hill, North Carolina

Preface

The Dow Jones average had just soared 250 points on the news that U.S. unemployment was at a 30-year low. The American economy entered yet another consecutive month of unprecedented expansion. Memories of the Cold War were rapidly fading. The political "third way" espoused by the erstwhile liberal leaders of the United States, Britain, Canada, Germany, and elsewhere—socially left-of-center yet fiscally conservative—was hailed as a model not only for the industrialized democratic world but for former socialist nations and "Third World" countries, as well. Approaching the last year of his presidency with his impeachment behind him, President Clinton sought to put an international stamp of approval on his legacy. As the leader of the nation with the most powerful economy in history, he headed for Seattle to give a valedictory address to the World Trade Organization (WTO) at a meeting largely orchestrated by his advisers and allies. Everone anticipated concurrence and accolades from trade ministers and stock-trading floors around the world.

But a funny thing happened on the way to the victory party. In what *The Economist* (Divan & Thorson, 1999, pp. 18-19) characterized as an "NGO (nongovernmental organization) swarm," union activists, environmentalists, and others around the world had become increasingly concerned about the universal adoption of unfettered capitalism. By this time, the NGOs were well experienced in forcing changes on seemingly omnipotent institutions. From pushing through agreements on greenhouse gases to outlawing landmines, to boycotting Nike for its labor practices, NGOs had developed an Internet-driven knack for establishing temporary or permanent coalitions to advocate various causes. Now, the WTO was being targeted: The massive protest organized via the Internet told WTO members that they would have to learn to sustain the prosperity of rich nations and export it to poorer ones without exporting barbaric labor conditions[1] and environmental destruction. By the time President Clinton made his way to the convention hall, Seattle had essentially been shut down by protests and anarchy in its streets. In his speech, Clinton rapidly backed off his bolder ideas for further opening world trade. WTO delegates left the riot-torn city frustrated and empty-handed.

Is this the new modus operandi for social change in the 21st century? Not necessarily. Some issues, such as the control of vaccine-preventable diseases, malaria, and acute respiratory infections, are not as emotionally compelling as land mines, even though these diseases kill and disable at vastly greater rates than left-over military ordnance. AIDS and tobacco-related diseases, finally being brought partially under control in wealthier nations, devastate the health and society of the planet's poorer regions at an ever-accelerating pace. Yet, the confrontation of the WTO in Seattle showed us that action can be taken to tackle some of the Earth's most intractable problems, even when the powerful establishment has to be confronted in the process. Rapid and effective communication combined with old-fashioned community organization and advocacy have revitalized efforts at effecting universal health and social change. An examination of how such change can be brought about will engage behavioral and social scientists for years to come.

Behavior Change and Public Health in the Developing World focuses on universal public health issues, how they developed, what can be done about them, and what the future holds. The book has two intended audiences. Students, researchers, and practitioners of health psychology, health education, and other health behavior-change endeavors, who may have had limited exposure to public health issues in developing countries, comprise the first group. The second audience consists of professionals and trainees in international public health, who perhaps have had limited exposure to health behavior-change theories and applications.

This is not a presentation of research methodologies nor of the disciplines that underpin them (epidemiology, demography, ethnography, and so forth). Rather, it emphasizes experience in behavior-change programs for the prevention and control of the world's biggest killers: malnutrition, respiratory infections, diarrhea, vaccine-preventable diseases, wasteful fertility, HIV/AIDS, and tobacco use. These programs are linked to theories and models that most typically frame them: health communications and social marketing, learning theory, media advocacy, and community self-control. Descriptions of programs and related literature presented in the book were selected essentially for how well they represent the application of a theory to a specific health or disease target.

This eight-chapter text comprises three basic sections. The first two chapters describe the overall international health picture, draw the association between health (or illness) and behavior, and present four basic theories or models of behavior change most applicable to the context of developing countries. The next five chapters provide details with respect to five "dependent variable" areas (malnutrition, infectious diseases, family planning, HIV/AIDS, and tobacco use) and present applications of the aforementioned behavior-change theories for addressing these public health issues. The final chapter addresses the accomplishments and shortcomings of behavior-change intervention experiences to date and looks at possible directions the field could or should take in the coming decades. Each chapter finishes with a summary and suggestions for additional readings.

The literature reviewed has been limited to that published in English- or Spanish-language (primarily peer-reviewed) journals or books that are available in university libraries. I reviewed the contents of recent editions of a wide variety of journals that frequently or exclusively present developing-country health issues. Internet sources pointed the way toward other publications, which were then tracked down by research assistants.

Unfortunately, many of the field's most practiced experts are not heard from here. Although I have endeavored to review research done in developing countries by developing-country investigators, many journals published in Asia, Africa, or Latin America were not available or were not abstracted on the Internet. Often, valuable experiences never get archived, as staff from field projects simply do not have that as a priority, nor do they have the resources or time to communicate their results in journal or book form. In other cases, experiences are written up in reports that, although valuable, are not accessible in any systematic fashion. Although my public health experience has been substantial, I would not make any sweeping claims with respect to my expertise. With respect to regions and health problems with which I have had minimal experience, I relied relatively more on the published word, whether through archived research or technical reports that I have persuaded colleagues to share with me. I apologize in advance to international experts who feel that, in my review, I have overlooked an important project (and I look forward to hearing from them about their work). I hope that the overall message of the text, nevertheless, will come through clearly.

The Swarm in Seattle showed that seemingly unstoppable social forces can at least be altered in form. But no one should be left with the impression that the momentum toward globalization has in any important way been weakened—indeed, it took a global effort to engineer the Seattle protest. Like economics and the media, public health has rapidly assumed an international character. As diseases refuse to respect national boundaries, neither can their prevention. *Behavior Change and Public Health in the Developing World* places the valuable lessons learned in chronic disease prevention in a universal context and explores new frontiers for the evolving technologies of behavior change and public health promotion.

▓ NOTE

1. Not all protestors, of course, were necessarily selfless in motive: Many simply did not want to see jobs leave the United States and other industrialized countries for poorer nations (Krauthammer, 1999).

Acknowledgments

This manuscript is the product of 15 years of work with numerous talented colleagues throughout the world. I owe my beginnings in international health to students and colleagues in nearby Tijuana, Mexico, most notably Rafael Laniado and Rene Salgado. For a decade, it was my honor to work with the American and international staff of the worldwide Health Communications for Child Survival (HealthCom) Project and its abundance of talent, including Bette Booth, Judy Graeff, Bill Smith, Terry Louis, Mark Rasmusson, Will Shaw, Patricio Barriga, Pepe Romero, Tom Reis, Andy Pillar, and many others. Later, I was privileged to collaborate with Lourdes Rivas, Linda Lloyd, Mark Nichter, and Gary Clark in the Yúcatan on a dengue-fever control project. Many of the ideas represented in this book were initially suggested by or developed in tandem with these people and others, and I am deeply indebted to all.

Equally valuable assistance came from other quarters as well. Jim Brace-Thompson from Sage has been a very supportive editor and got me through some of the rough spots. Jacqueline Tasch and Nevair Kabakian of Sage were also central to the editing and production process. Connie Elder, Rick Gersberg, Jim Sallis, and four anonymous reviewers arranged for by Sage provided indispensable editorial advice, helping transform a very rough draft into a finished product. Rick Gersberg and Susan Wilson also served as an important sounding board for the "Wheel of Disease" concept. Ken Bart provided critical information on immunization campaigns. Susan Zimicki updated me on some promising initiatives of the CHANGE Project. Esther Martínez, April Busic, and Sunny Choe carried out much of the library work, and Veronica Serrano, Lisa Kondrat, and Nancy Phu prepared the graphs. Jenny Offner, Nancy Phu, and Amelia Arroyo processed the manuscript into a presentable form. The excellent library resources of the Escuela Nacional de Sanidad in Madrid, Spain, proved critical for later revisions. I would like to thank Dean José María Martín Moreno and Professors Antonio Sarría and María Teresa García of the Escuela Nacional de Sanidad for hosting me during my wonderful year in Spain.

Sabbaticals are critical times of renewal for university faculty, and I would like to express my appreciation to San Diego State University (SDSU) for granting me the 1-year leave during which I wrote this manuscript. Nevertheless, responsibilities do not simply disappear for a year, and I am indebted to many SDSU colleagues for filling in for me during my absence. Mel Hovell, Joni Mayer, Moshe Engelberg, Greg Talavera, and Terry Conway accepted most of my teaching assignments during my absence. Amelia Arroyo, Nadia Campbell, Jeanette Candelaria, Suchi Ayala, Don Slymen, and Al Litrownik, among others, had to fill in for me in various research and administrative capacities. Although I am sure some of them are thinking "He owes me!," I never heard a word of complaint from any of them.

This effort was, in part, inspired by many enjoyable Sunday morning conversations with Dale Daniel. A renowned surgeon with a public health soul, he never failed to speak out for peace, equality, and the protection of the environment, and he stimulated all who knew him to do the same.

—John P. Elder
Madrid, Spain
April 7, 2000

1

Health Behavior
in the Developing World

░

Background

░ ░ The now-maturing disciplines of health psychology and behavioral medi-
░ ░ cine have historically emphasized behavior change for chronic disease prevention. Thus, smoking cessation, dietary cholesterol and fat reduction, weight
loss, physical activity, and stress management comprised the initial subject matter
of this emerging field, as the links between human behavior and mortality due to
heart disease and cancer became clear. In the mid-1980s, the outbreak of the
AIDS epidemic compelled us to broaden our horizons to include infectious diseases. Nevertheless, our primary targets have not changed substantially since the
launching of the North Karelia and Stanford Five City Projects nearly three decades ago. As a discipline, health psychology, like other behavioral sciences,
largely emphasizes diseases more prevalent in adults living in affluent societies.

Worldwide, however, children and young women are far more likely to suffer and die than are older adults, a pattern that has been true since the beginning of
history. Some developing countries in East Asia and Latin America have experienced favorable changes in this trend, but elsewhere—particularly in some coun-

tries in Africa and South Asia—no progress has been realized. Maurice King (1991) argued that with overpopulation and the collapse of the environment, infant and child mortality rates due to malnutrition and disease could explode in the near future. Overpopulation and habitat destruction may actually speed the emergence of "new" diseases (such as Ebola and hantavirus) and others previously thought to be under control (e.g., tuberculosis, dengue fever).

Human behavior change holds the key to improving child survival and other indices of global health, as it does for chronic disease prevention. Although health psychologists have chosen to target the latter, health behavior-change techniques can be melded with interventions shown to be effective in international arenas for dramatic relief of suffering worldwide. This newly integrated approach will have only a limited effect if behavioral issues related to population growth, consumption, and equality are not addressed concurrently with child survival and general health. In a related way, sustained improvements can only be accomplished within the context of broader environmental, policy, and community change.

As its interrelation with the broader field of public health is articulated, however, the discipline of health psychology will increasingly find itself addressing more universal and complex problems. The complementary purposes of this book are to demonstrate the relevance of international health issues to health psychology as well as the utility of a health behavior-change technology to developers of international health programs.

A Brief History of the Discipline of Public Health

George Rosen's (1993) classic *A History of Public Health* traces the roots of modern public health practices to five distinct periods. During the Greco-Roman period, the foundations were laid for the medical profession (Greek), use of engineering to ensure a safe water supply, sewage management efforts, and public health administration (Roman). Greek medicine was characterized by relatively strong scientific thought and empirical observations, predated in this regard only by Chinese and Indian medical practice (Basch, 1999).

The Middle Ages witnessed the growth of urban areas and the concomitant need to deal with sanitation problems; hospitals were developed, and specific administrative measures were created to deal with health matters such as quarantines, all in the context of a generally superstitious and anti-intellectual society (Rosen, 1993). The Black Death and other plagues, killing large proportions of the world's population in the 14th and 15th centuries, led to some of the earliest efforts in the international public health arena, including the quarantine of ships in Venice and other Mediterranean ports (Basch, 1999, pp. 22-23).

In the age of Mercantilism and Absolutism (1500-1750), great advances in science led, among other things, to a renaissance in medicine, the precise recognition of diseases, and a quantitative approach to health problems. (As discussed in Chapter 7, perhaps the greatest plague of all time has its roots in this period, as well: the exposure of Spanish, English, and other sailors to New World tobacco and its subsequent export to Europe and beyond).

During the Enlightenment and Revolutionary period (until 1830), political and intellectual leaders rededicated themselves to the betterment of humanity. Efforts were undertaken to diminish the toll of child mortality, anti-alcohol campaigns were initiated, and sanitariums and dispensaries were founded. During this era, Lind demonstrated the role of diet in the prevention of scurvy, and Jenner discovered the smallpox vaccine. Societies began to awaken to the human costs of industrialization and urbanization (Rosen, 1993).

Rosen (1993) labels the next 45 years as the era of industrialism and the sanitary movement. Theories of human miasma and divine interventions were replaced by laboratory observations and biological formulations, catalyzed by the publications on evolution by Darwin (Basch, 1991). During this time, European and American scientists and officials realized the exact nature of communicable diseases and began to mandate the removal of garbage, construction of drainage, and provision of safe water. Strict scientific approaches to research became the norm. Finally, improvements in epidemiological methods, laboratory technology, and international communication launched the bacteriological era (circa 1875), with incontrovertible evidence of the association between micro-organisms and disease and a proliferation of effective preventive measures for infections. With the onset of the bacteriological era, public health became subsumed under the general field of medicine, more or less as a subdiscipline on an equal footing with internal medicine, surgery, pediatrics, and other medical specialties (McKinlay & Marceau, 2000).

Since the end of Rosen's chronology a half century ago, we need another label to characterize more recent developments in the field. The history of public health is extraordinarily rich and varied. However, virtually all of the eras described by Rosen have an element in common: Although revolutionaries, researchers, and physicians all had active roles in changing the health of societies, the people actually meant to benefit from these changes were perceived to be passive leaves being blown about by alternating winds of illness and health. Beginning with the publication of the Lalonde (1974) report, *A New Perspective on the*

Health of Canadians, this perception truly became history. Several writers including Ashton (1992) have labeled the past three decades the "New Public Health" era, defined as

> an approach which draws crucially from the environmental, personal, preventive, and therapeutic eras and seeks a synthesis. Its focus is on public policy as well as on individual behavior and lifestyle and increasingly it is being seen in an ecological context which has a focus on holistic health. (p. 4)

As is evident, a key emphasis of this New Public Health era is health behavior and the environment in which it occurs, beginning with the focus on behavioral risk factors for heart disease, lung cancer, and other chronic diseases and now extending even to the link between human activity and infectious diseases, environmental damage, and population. In the New Public Health era, both societies and individuals have to take responsibility for health, rather than waiting for changes to be made for them. The study of health behavior, therefore, must be considered under the broader umbrella of public health, which, in turn, would no longer be a component of medicine but an independent multidisciplinary field (McKinlay & Marceau, 2000). Such is the primary subject matter for this book.

The Global Burden of Disease

Until the last decade, there was no systematic worldwide attempt to quantify health problems of populations. Although the ability to calculate fertility rates and demographic trends and projections is fairly sophisticated (Murray & Lopez, 1996), public health has typically relied on crude mortality rates as an indicator of the impact of disease in the world, a straightforward description of how many people are dying at what age and from what cause. This presents a partial rather than total picture of the impact of disease on populations, as high rates of illness may actually cripple a country more than high death rates.

The Global Burden of Disease Study was initiated in 1992 by the World Bank and the World Health Organization to "foster an independent, evidence-based approach to public health policy formulation" (Murray & Lopez, 1996, p. 740). *Burden of disease* is a conceptual representation of the difference between the ideal and true health of a population. Manifested as a function of the frequency, duration, and severity of illnesses affecting a population, this burden can actually be quantified, using coefficients such as disability-adjusted life years (DALYs). Burden of disease estimates may assist in planning health services, prioritizing various health interventions, and estimating economic losses or gains due to diseases and their control (World Bank, 1997, p. 28).

Table 1.1 presents both overall mortality rates and DALYs figures for the 11 leading causes of death worldwide (adapted from Murray & Lopez, 1997a, 1997b). As is shown in the two left columns, chronic diseases such as ischemic heart disease, cerebrovascular disease, chronic obstructive pulmonary disease, and cancer are major killers throughout the world, with the former two ranking first and second. These are followed by infectious diseases and perinatal problems, far more likely to threaten populations in underdeveloped countries.[1] Yet, overall mortality presents just part of the picture, as chronic diseases are more likely to strike elderly individuals, who may have already lived long and productive lives; reductions in chronic disease are more likely to benefit wealthier rather than poorer nations (Gwatkin, Guillot, & Heuveline, 1999). DALYs,[2] defined as "future years of disability-free life that are lost as the result of the premature deaths or cases of disability occurring in a particular year" (Basch, 1999, p. 108) calculates mortality adjusted by age and morbidity adjusted by both age and its severity. (For example, a 35-year-old killed in an auto accident would have lost about 40 DALYs, the same number as an infant passenger in the car who was disabled about 50% by the accident). In terms of the ranking of DALYs, the three most severe problems worldwide become respiratory infections, diarrhea, and perinatal disease, due especially to their impact on the very young. All of the other

TABLE 1.1 Leading Causes of Death Worldwide and Disability Adjusted Life Years (DALYs), 1990

Deaths (Rank)	Number of Deaths (in 1,000s)	Cause	DALYs (Rank)
1	6,260	Ischemic heart disease	5
2	4,381	Stroke	6
3	4,299	Lower respiratory infections	1
4	2,946	Diarrhea	2
5	2,443	Perinatal disorders	3
6	2,211	Chronic obstructive pulmonary disease	12
7	1,960	Tuberculosis	7
8	1,058	Measles	8
9	999	Road traffic accidents	9
10	945	Cancer (lung, trachea, bronchus)[a]	
11	856	Malaria	11

a. Cancer is a major killer but not a major cause of disability, because death (or in some cases full recovery) is relatively quick. Therefore, it ranks far lower as a producer of DALYs than the other diseases listed.

major killers and producers of disability, except for road accidents, are substantially or nearly entirely related to cigarette smoking.

The Universality of Health Behavior

In underdeveloped countries millions of people, most of them very young, die or suffer every year from largely preventable health problems. As there is a behavioral and not purely biological or medical genesis to many of these problems, the application of health psychology to public health in these countries is as relevant as its application to chronic diseases and other issues in more affluent nations. Clearly, societal factors such as per capita income, the distribution of income, education, gender equality, and human rights, and governmental expenditures on food, water, and sanitation contribute significantly to morbidity and mortality (see Chapter 8). However, behavior-change technology may provide critical contributions to the conceptualization and implementation of public health promotion programs in the developing as well as the developed world (Elder, Schmid, Hovell, Molgaard, & Graeff, 1989).

Underdeveloped nations in Africa, Asia, and Latin America suffer from a different pattern of morbidity and mortality than do their Western (i.e., largely northern) counterparts. Children in the poorest countries of Africa and Asia are 20 times more likely to die before their fifth birthday than are children born in the United States (Elder, Geller, Hovell, & Mayer, 1994). Infectious diseases, vector-born diseases, parasitic diseases, malnutrition, and wasteful fertility[3] portend the continuance of these problems for the foreseeable future, in spite of recent gains. HIV/AIDS and other emerging or re-emerging diseases can quickly wipe out hard-won improvements in child survival and other health areas. These international realities are gradually shaping a broader health behavior focus in the field of public health promotion.

Facts for Life (UNICEF, 1991) presents the critical challenges to international public health in terms of "prime messages" that organize health behavior-change thinking. These messages are categorized in the following tables into family planning, nutrition, and the prevention and control of infectious diseases. The specific behavioral targets include birth timing and safe motherhood (Table 1.2), breast-feeding and child growth (Table 1.3), diarrhea and the management of respiratory infections (Table 1.4), and immunizations, home hygiene, vector control, and AIDS (Table 1.5).

The achievement of the behavior-change goals explicit or implicit in these prime messages would greatly alleviate the global burden of disease and shift some of it from the shoulders of the planet's poorest people.

TABLE 1.2 Key Messages for Family Planning and Reproductive Health

- Becoming pregnant before 18 or after 35 increases health risks for both mother and child.
- Birth spacing of less than 2 years increases mortality risk for young children by 50%.
- Having more than four children in total increases the health risks of pregnancy and childbirth.
- Regular checkups during pregnancy reduce risks related to childbirth.
- A trained birth attendant should assist at every birth.
- All families should know warning signs of various dangers of pregnancy and childbirth.
- All women need more food and rest during pregnancy.
- Family planning is the best approach to ensuring that couples can choose when to begin having children, how many to have, how much to space births, and when to stop having

TABLE 1.3 Key Messages for Breast-Feeding and Nutrition

- Breast milk alone is the best possible baby food during the first 4 to 6 months of life, and breast-feeding should continue well into the second year of a child's life or even longer.
- Babies should begin breast-feeding as soon as possible after birth. Nearly every mother should be able to breast-feed.
- Supplemental foods are needed at the end of the breast milk-alone period.
- Bottle feeding can lead to serious illnesses or even death.
- Children between the ages of 6 months and 3 years should be weighed every month for growth monitoring. If there is no weight gain for 2 months, this is cause for concern.
- Children under 3 years of age need to be fed five or six times a day and more frequently after illnesses.
- Children under 3 years of age need a small amount of extra fat or oil added to the family's ordinary food.
- Parents should feed their children food rich in vitamin A.

Epidemiology and Health Psychology

The Roots of Behavioral Epidemiology

Many benefits could be gained from closer links between the study of health behavior and public health's central discipline, epidemiology. Epidemiology, the study of the distribution and determinants of diseases in humans, is typically only indirectly addressed in clinically or behaviorally oriented disciplines such as health psychology. Such a lack of articulation between these two fields is unfortu-

TABLE 1.4 Key Messages for Control of Infectious Diseases:
Diarrhea and Acute Respiratory Infections

Diarrhea

- Diarrhea can kill children through dehydration. Therefore, children with diarrhea need plenty of liquids to drink.
- When children have diarrhea, it is important to continue regular breast-feeding or other feeding.
- If diarrhea becomes serious, trained medical attention is necessary.
- Children recovering from diarrhea need extra feeding opportunities.
- Generally, medicine should not be used to treat diarrhea, unless specifically prescribed by a physician.
- Oral rehydration solutions can be especially effective in treating dehydration due to diarrhea.

Acute Respiratory Infections

- Children who have coughs and are breathing much more rapidly than normal should be taken for medical attention quickly.
- Children with coughs or colds should be encouraged to eat regularly and drink plenty of fluids.
- Children with coughs or colds should be kept warm and should not be exposed to smoke or contaminated air.

nate for a variety of reasons. First, behavioral scientists need to be able to determine what true public health priorities are so that they can validate or alter their own research and practice efforts. Behavior-change experts need to be aware of where the overall health field is headed and update their skills or acquire new specializations accordingly. Even if behavioral specialists choose to address areas of inquiry of limited population significance, acquiring at least the language of epidemiology will allow them to communicate their activities to a much larger audience.

Second, epidemiology offers important research techniques normally not presented in behavioral science curricula. For example, epidemiology anticipated subsequent research in behavioral psychology in terms of the calculation of interrater reliability in behavioral observation. While behaviorists grappled with whether to represent the reliability of observations as percentage agreement, percentage disagreement, or some combination of the two (cf. Wallace & Elder, 1980), the conceptual and mathematical approaches for quantifying reliability had already been developed within the field of clinical epidemiology. Specifically, statistics related to assessing the quality of screening procedures, such as

TABLE 1.5 Key Messages for the Prevention of Infectious Diseases: Immunization, Hygiene, Vector Control, and HIV

Immunization

- All parents should know that immunization protects against several dangerous diseases. Children not immunized are far more likely to become malnourished, suffer from disability, or die.
- All immunization should be completed in the first year of the child's life. Parents should not delay having their children immunized.
- It is completely safe to immunize a sick child.
- Women of childbearing age should be fully immunized against tetanus.

Hygiene

- Illnesses can be prevented by washing hands with soap and water after contact with fecal matter and especially before handling food.
- Illness can be prevented by using latrines.
- Illnesses can also be prevented by using water from a safe source, especially bottled or boiled water.
- Illness can be prevented by boiling drinking water if it is not from a safe pipe supply.
- Keeping food clean can also prevent illness. Household refuse should be disposed of carefully, often by burying it.

Vector Control

- All people, especially young children, should be protected from mosquito bites and other vector contact.
- Individuals should work together with their communities to destroy vectors (e.g., through the destruction of mosquito larvae) and prevent mosquitoes from breeding by eliminating breeding sites.

HIV/AIDS

- AIDS is an incurable disease that can be passed on via sexual intercourse, infected blood, and infected mothers to their unborn and newly born children.
- Safe sex is the primary method of preventing HIV infections. Remaining monogamous, making sure that neither partner in a relationship is infected, and using a condom if HIV status is in any doubt are all effective methods of practicing safe sex.
- Any use of an unsterilized needle or syringe is dangerous. Unclean metal objects that penetrate the skin may spread the HIV virus.
- Women with the AIDS virus should avoid becoming pregnant

the calculation of sensitivity and specificity, parallel those for reliability coefficients (percentage agreement and percentage disagreement).

Thus, behaviorists who are well versed in epidemiology can, at a minimum, avoid reinventing the wheel. More important, epidemiology's perspectives on research designs and techniques will enrich the field of health psychology. Ewart

(1991) noted that the fields of epidemiology and public health have for many decades sought to advance disease control and enhance quality of life (dating back to simple examinations of who became sick and when and where they did so); by doing so, they have helped determine preventive measures before biological host-disease mechanisms were even determined. Ewart also joined in the criticism of "victim-blaming" individual or clinical interventions, which seek to alter unhealthy lifestyles in the face of illness-creating physical, social, and political environments. In turn, psychology has much to offer the fields of epidemiology and public health. Questionnaire development, interviewing approaches, behavioral observation techniques, and behavior-change methodologies are all sets of skills prevalent among psychologists and other behavioral scientists.

The cross-fertilization of epidemiology with behavioral sciences is manifested by the emerging field of behavioral epidemiology, which may be defined as the study of (a) the distribution of health-related behaviors in populations; (b) the association of these behaviors with health, morbidity, and mortality; and (c) techniques for changing these behaviors on a population-wide basis. Increasingly, epidemiologists are discovering the behavioral connection with virtually all major threats to the health of humans, from chronic diseases and disabilities to infectious diseases and habitat destruction.

Magnitude of Effect

The obverse of the burden of disease coin is the concept of magnitude of effect. With the application of behavior-change technology to public health issues has come a realization of the value of scale. Public health, with its roots in medicine, has been faulted for too often emphasizing the small portion of the population at extremely high risk: in other words, the tail end of the distribution rather than the entire population curve (McKinlay & Marceau, 1999). For example, the census-based, impact-oriented (CBIO) approach for strengthening health programs in developing countries (Perry et al., 1999) includes as one of its tenets "identifying those persons who are at greatest risk of developing [illness or risk] conditions, and providing appropriate preventive or curative services to these 'targeted' community members" (p. 1055). In contrast, Geoffrey Rose (1992) asserts that small changes in an entire population will result in greater public health changes than large changes in a small group of high-risk individuals. In small-group or individual efforts, effects have to be large to ensure clinical significance. However, in population-based interventions, smaller success rates still would mean that large numbers of people might benefit from a particular intervention.

For example, a 70% condom-adoption rate in the patient population of a sexually transmitted disease (STD) clinic may be deemed successful, yet, it would not do much to lower overall community risk, whereas a 10% adoption rate in this same high-risk subgroup would probably be considered an abject failure. In contrast, a mass media campaign to promote condom use in an entire community that produced a 10% effect would be deemed an extraordinary success. Even if the magnitude of effect is not as great as has been found for highly focused applications, the use of modestly powerful interventions in large populations can still produce important improvements for the population as a whole. The use of powerful intervention techniques with a relatively small group of individuals may increase the magnitude of effect from a population perspective; however, a broader based intervention applied to larger populations would be more likely to do so, even if the resulting intervention is less intensive at the individual level (Elder et al., 1989).

The Jakarta Declaration

Such broad-based interventions have been emphasized by international health organizations for over two decades. Beginning with the Alma Ata Conference in 1978 and followed by the Ottawa Charter on Health Promotion in 1987 and the subsequent Jakarta Declaration in 1997, the World Health Organization and its members have asserted that health is a basic human right and essential for social and economic development. According to these declarations, prerequisites for health are peace, shelter, education, social security, the empowerment of women, a stable ecosystem, sustainable resource use, social justice, respect for human rights, and equity. Worldwide social, political, and economic forces—urbanization, an integrated global economy, and access to media and technology—dictate that any health actions be flexible as well as forceful. Drug abuse, resistance to antibiotics, environmental degradation, and an increase in the number of older people demand new strategies as well as refinements in previously proven ones (Pan American Health Organization/World Health Organization, 1986; World Health Organization, 1978).

Simply mounting programs to address the behavioral aspects of the world's most destructive diseases will, at most, yield a temporary improvement. Idealistic in tone, the Jakarta Declaration's health promotion priorities nevertheless are highly consistent with the New Public Health focus described above, placing our behavior-change strategies into a context for future efforts. According to this declaration, health promotion programs should accomplish the following:

1. Promote social responsibility for health. Both public and private sectors should promote health by pursuing policies and practices that avoid harming the health of others; protect the environment and sustainable use of resources; restrict production and trade in inherently harmful goods and substances such as tobacco and arms, as well as unhealthy marketing practices; safeguard both the citizen in the marketplace and the individual in the workplace; and include equity-focused health impact assessments as an integral part of policy development.

2. Increase investments for health development. Additional resources for education, housing, and the health sector must be forthcoming. Greater investment in health and reorientation of existing investments have the potential to significantly advance human development, health, and quality of life. This investment must reflect the needs of relatively disempowered groups such as women, children, older people, and indigenous, poor, and/or marginalized populations.

3. Consolidate and expand partnerships for health. Health promotion requires partnerships at all levels of government and society.

4. Increase community capacity and empower the individual. Health promotion is carried out by and with people, not on or to people. It improves both the ability of individuals to take action and the capacity of groups, organizations, or communities to influence the determinants of health. Improving the capacity of communities to foster health promotion requires practical education, leadership training, and access to resources. Empowering individuals requires more reliable and consistent access to the decision-making process and skills and knowledge essential to effect change.

5. Secure an infrastructure for health promotion. New mechanisms of local, national, and global funding must be found.

Incentives should be developed to influence the actions of governments, nongovernmental organizations (NGOs), educational institutions, and the private sector to make sure that resource mobilization for health promotion is maximized. New health challenges mean that new and diverse networks need to be created to achieve intersectoral collaboration. Such networks should provide mutual assistance within and between countries and facilitate exchange of information on which strategies are effective in which settings.

Training of local leadership should be encouraged to support health promotion activities. Documentation of experiences in health promotion through consumer-friendly research and project reporting should be enhanced to improve planning, implementation, and evaluation.

Birth timing, safe motherhood breast-feeding, child growth, diarrhea control, the management of respiratory infections, immunizations, home hygiene, vector control, and AIDS will continue to garner the attention of international health efforts for years to come. However, the Jakarta Declaration and its predecessors anticipate the need to focus more broadly away from such single disease or health issues to tackle more "upstream" factors through health promotion efforts. Although specific health-promotion priority targets are emphasized in the document (including health-promoting clinical services, healthy schools, healthy workplaces, tobacco-free societies, healthy homes and families, and sexual health), the techniques for accomplishing these efforts were left vague at best. Without a firm theoretical and practical grounding in behavioral targets, be they at the individual, community, or decision-maker level, calls to action represented by the Jakarta Declaration will encounter difficulty moving away from being much more than that.

SUMMARY

The field of public health has evolved from an emphasis on sanitation and the isolation of diseased individuals to a dynamic science that explores and seeks to remedy specific causes of illness. We are currently in an era of behavioral health, in which human behavior is looked at as a source of chronic disease risk factors and their prevention. In addition, vaccinations, breast-feeding and nutrition, the management of childhood diarrhea and acute respiratory infections, family planning,

Children in a migrant labor camp in Latin America: An expansion of health promotion targets to address upstream issues is needed.

home hygiene, vector control, and the prevention of the spread of HIV infections all have direct behavior-change implications. With an emphasis on such behaviors, individuals, communities, and societies must be given the responsibility and capacity for maintaining their health and that of their families and neighbors.

FURTHER READING

Basch, P. F. (1999). *Textbook of international health* (2nd ed.). New York: Oxford University Press.

Brown, S. (Ed.). *State of the world* [annual review]. New York: Norton.

Notes

1. As Gwatkin et al. (1999) points out, the poorest 20% of the world's countries would benefit 10 times as much as the richest nations from substantial reductions in communicable diseases, whereas the richest 20% would gain 4 times as much as the poorest from comparable reductions in noncommunicable diseases.

2. DALYs, an improvement over crude mortality rates, still cannot totally represent the public health picture. HIV/AIDS, for example, not quite yet on the list of major killers, leaves in its wake not only adults who suffer horribly before they die but also their orphans, who as described in Chapter 6, are the fastest-growing population of many African cities.

3. Wasteful fertility involves pregnancies or childbirths that are unwanted, as well as those the compromise the health of the mother, baby, or other members of the family. Such health problems are often related to a high level of parity, inadequate food supplies or medical services, or dangerous abortion procedures. Indirectly, wasteful fertility can threaten entire communities where financial or environmental resources are inadequate to sustain high birth rates.

2

A Few Good Theories—and Behavioral Interventions That Work

Kurt Lewin's axiom that there is nothing so useful as a good theory takes on a special meaning for public health behavior-change programs in developing countries. Indeed, public health's flagship discipline, epidemiology, has been faulted by McKinlay and Marceau (2000) for a lack of theory development: "Established epidemiology can actually explain very little, because in epidemiology, unlike most disciplines, there is little interest in developing theories that can be tested" (p. 26). Health psychology and other behavioral sciences, in contrast, judge interventions and other research on both (a) the amount of individual behavior change achieved and (b) the extent to which broader generalizations can be made to other behavior-change efforts and phenomena, largely as a function of whether the intervention and evaluation were theory driven.

Yet, many theories and models current in the behavioral field would share McKinlay and Marceau's (2000) criticisms of epidemiology for being reductionistic, individualistic, and driven to some extent by biomedicine. These theories and models of behavior change, thus, have limited applicability to public health behavior-change efforts, especially those in the developing world.

Popular psychosocial theories are predicated on Western notions of individual autonomy and purpose. Concepts such as *reasoned action* and *behavioral intentions*—as applied to individuals—may hold less relevance for populations in traditional communal cultures, where individual identity is grounded in family and community roles (e.g., King et al., 1995). Second, many theories imply or require detailed, thorough individual measurement, making them less practical for people who are not accustomed to such instrumentation or who have limited literacy, or for programs with no resources for such measurement. Western psychologically based theories are often more connected to the understanding of individual cognitive processes than to intervention design per se. As applied to health, they are more suited to interventions for small, high-risk segments of populations than for entire populations (Cohen, Scribner, & Farley, 2000; McKinlay & Marceau, 1999).

In the context of general ecological theory, Cohen et al. (2000) propose a structural model of health behavior change. Four specific factors delineated within this model are availability, physical structures, social structures, and cultural and media messages. Availability refers to how accessible health-related consumer products are (e.g., vitamin A-rich foods, over-the-counter medications, condoms, and cigarettes). Physical structures are those aspects of products or environments that make health-related behavior more or less likely to occur (e.g., single-use needles for IV drug users, good roads and transportation to health clinics, or mobile screening and immunization services). Social structures refer to laws and policies that require or restrict health behaviors and to their enforcement (e.g., restrictions on tobacco sales and where it can be consumed, immunization requirements for enrolling in public schools). Informal social control mechanisms (e.g., nonsmokers asserting their rights to a smoke-free environment) are central to this category as well. Finally, cultural and media messages are those to which individuals are exposed every day (e.g., health messages and alcohol beverage ads) and that inform them about specific health behaviors and denote social norms underpinning these behaviors.

Cohen and her colleagues (2000) argue that these four factors represent a blueprint for most or all of effective public health behavior-change interventions. Of special interest is the fact that only the final (cultural/media) of the four factors in any way implies that knowledge and attitude change can occur before behavior change. Although not presented as a psychosocial theory itself, this structural model does bring into question the validity of emphasizing personality and cognitions in efforts to study and change public health behaviors.

Health communications (specifically, the communications-persuasion model) and learning theory are less linked to individual personality constructs or to hypothesized cognitive processes, and are, thus, less culturally bound. In addition, these two theories provide specific blueprints for behavior-change interventions and have been tried and proven useful in developing-country contexts. These practical theories, along with integrative media advocacy and community self-control models, provide the foundation for the intervention approaches described in this book.

Health Communications and Social Marketing

Central to the field of health communications is McGuire's (1981) communication-persuasion model, which presents an input-output matrix to describe stages (outputs) leading to behavior change and how progress through these stages is aided by communication in its various forms (inputs). The inputs represent qualities of the communicated message that can be manipulated and controlled by campaign designers, whereas outputs represent the information-processing steps that must be stimulated in those receiving the message. Specifically, the inputs address "who says what, via what medium, to whom, directed at what kind of target" (p. 45). This translates into information regarding the source, the message, the channel, the receiver, and the destination. Source characteristics refer to the communicator of the message. Persuasive impact may be influenced by such factors as age, gender, ethnicity, credibility, and socioeconomic status. Message refers to the information that is communicated, and important factors include delivery style, content organization, length, and repetition. Channel comprises the mode of communication, including face-to-face, print (newspaper, brochures, etc.), and broadcast. Receiver characteristics include such variables as age, education, intelligence, and demographic variables considered when creating a public health campaign. Finally, the destination describes the targeted behaviors and issues to be considered, including long-term versus short-term change and specific versus general behaviors.

Outputs reflect the temporal process and stages of change from initial exposure to communication to long-term maintenance of change within the intended receiver. The 12 output steps progress as follows: exposure, attention, liking, comprehension, skill acquisition, attitude change, memory storage, information search and retrieval from memory, decision based on retrieval, behavior in accordance with decision, reinforcement, and consolidation. All of these are necessary for a given communication to be effective, and the theory assumes that these output-processing steps are contingent on each other and, therefore, must occur more or less in the specified sequence. A strength of McGuire's (1981) theory is that it lends itself both to program design and to evaluation of specific changes related to a communication effort. Several variations on this theory incorporate different output-processing routes, accounting for behavioral change leading to attitude change instead of vice versa or focusing on activation of information that is already possessed by the individual and increasing the salience of message components that support those current beliefs.

In important ways, the communication-persuasion model (especially its output dimension) parallels the widely used transtheoretical model (TTM) (Prochaska & DiClemente, 1983). In the TTM, stages represent the periods of time in which particular changes occur, as well as a continuum of readiness to take and sustain action (Elder, Ayala, Zabinski, Prochaska, & Gehrman, 2000). The TTM characterizes individuals as moving from precontemplation (not intending to change), to contemplation (intending to change in the near future), to preparation (actively planning immediate change), to action (overtly making changes), and finally to maintenance (taking steps to sustain change). To be considered in action, individuals are required to meet some behavioral criterion at least for some minimal period of time (e.g., 6 months), after which the individual enters the maintenance stage. The TTM conceptualizes change as a dynamic, nonlinear process, with the majority of people relapsing and returning to earlier stages of change before successfully reaching maintenance (Prochaska & DiClemente, 1998). More than the TTM, however, McGuire's (1981) conceptualization has guided the field of public health communication, especially in the use of mass media. This holds special relevance for health promotion in nations with large rural populations, where mass media must be relied on to a greater extent than in urban areas, where populations are concentrated and can be contacted relatively easily.

Public health communication includes a variety of techniques but specifically emphasizes a few practical and simple messages through as many channels as possible. The success of a communication program is determined by a variety of factors, including (a) how much access the target audience has to the information (e.g., does a large percentage of the target audience own televisions and radios?), (b) whether people were actually exposed to the media advertisement (e.g., did a poster in a health post stay up long enough for people to see it?), (c) whether the target audience acquired sufficient knowledge and skills to perform the target behavior (much more relevant for complex behaviors such as the safe operation of farm machinery than for relatively simple ones such as bringing a child in for immunizations), (d) whether the target audience actually has the opportunity to perform the behavior (e.g., new physical activity skills should be taught with reference to the appropriate season), and (e) whether this trial and subsequent short-term adoption can be reinforced naturally through subsequent communication approaches.

The Health Communication and Social Marketing Process

Social marketing integrates methods derived from the fields of business and health communication for changing socially relevant behavior (Bloom & Novelli, 1984). Applied specifically to health promotion, it has been used to (a) create awareness of a health issue, problem, or solution; (b) create demand for health services or even (as discussed later in this chapter) legislative action; (c) teach skills; and (d) prompt and reinforce the maintenance and generalization of beneficial behavior change (U.S. Department of Health and Human Services, 1989). Social marketing can be applied to achieving any of McGuire's (1981) outputs, especially the initial stages of getting people's attention and improving knowledge about a health issue.

Communication and social marketing plans lay out in general terms how marketing activities will be developed, implemented, and evaluated. This plan consists of market analysis, market segmentation, and marketing strategy (including lists of products/behaviors, message construction, creative approach, and marketing mix).

Market analysis. Marketing analysis consists of identifying who the target audience is and what we want them to do (Academy for Educational Development, 1995). It establishes the market "boundaries" (i.e., whom and what are to be targeted and excluded), the geographic area encompassed, and whether the market size is changing. Second, the market analysis obtains both demographic and "psychographic" information, the latter referring to the wants, needs, perceptions, attitudes, habits, readiness for change, and satisfaction levels of the target population. The important characteristics of targeted individuals or groups are derived from both primary data (gathered from questionnaires, focus groups, and interviews) and secondary data (obtained from archival investigation).

Segmentation. Market segmentation is the partitioning of a potential market into homogeneous subgroups based on the common characteristics identified in the market analysis. The purpose of market segmentation is to provide a basis for selecting primary and secondary audiences and developing optimal promotional programs for them. The criteria for selecting the primary audience are as follows: (a) who is most affected by the problem or issue, (b) which group would benefit most from the behavioral intervention, and (c) which group might be most responsive to the intervention. For the selection of the secondary audience, the following factors are considered: (a) who might use and reinforce the message to others (e.g., health workers) and (b) who might influence the primary audience to listen and respond to the messages (e.g., parents) (Academy for Educational Development, 1995).

Strategy. After social marketers analyze the market and determine target segments, they develop a specific marketing strategy to achieve the desired behavior change in the context of the interests and characteristics of the identified targets. A specific, central communication message consistent with program goals is decided on at this point. This message will be presented clearly and consistently in all subsequent promotion efforts, program materials, and products. Kotler's 4 Ps of marketing strategy are considered, including the development or diversification of the *product,* backed by *promotion,* and put in *place* at the right *price.* The implementation of specific strategies depends on the novelty of experience with the product or audience (Kotler & Andreasen, 1996; Kotler & Roberto, 1989).

While developing the product, the objective is to package the social idea in a manner that (a) is desirable to the target audience, (b) makes the audience willing to "purchase" (in terms of attitude or behavior change), and (c) facilitates the social cause. For example, nutritional health promotion programs must decide if their product consists of behaviors that prevent disease (e.g., eating green, leafy vegetables) or promote a healthier lifestyle in general (e.g., eating a fully-balanced diet with plentiful calories) or foster use of a specific nutritional substance (e.g., vitamin A supplements). In many cases, no single product can achieve the desired social change; various products and marketing strategies that contribute to the social objective must be developed.

Product positioning refers to the selection of a niche in the marketplace for a product or behavior, taking into account both the needs and wants of consumers and whatever competition may exist. For example, the promotion of oral rehydration solutions is done with the realization that mothers use home remedies and other products (some of which are dangerous) in response to their baby's diarrhea.

Another important factor to consider in product development is the price of the product. The price represents the cost to the buyer, including monetary expenditure, time, and energy. For example, the costs of oral rehydration therapy may include the monetary charge for ORS packets, the fuel or time required to boil water, and the psychological cost of worrying about whether the solution was mixed appropriately.

Next, we need to determine where and in what situation (e.g., time of day/day of week) we can best reach our target audiences. Promoting breast-feeding on daytime television may be a good way to reach housewives, whereas women in the workforce may be more easily reached through print media at the work site. Thus, *place* refers to providing adequate distribution and response channels whereby the social idea can reach the relevant public. A distribution network should be established that will (a) permit implementation of the social change effort on a broad scale, (b) facilitate communication between the change agents and recipients, and (c) expedite the desired behavior change.

Finally, the promotion of the product includes both the creative approach and media mix. The creativity of a marketing approach may greatly influence how much attention people pay to the message delivered. Within the findings of their research, marketers apply their creativity in developing

1. The content of the message
2. The product position
3. The tone of the message—whether comforting or alarming, intellectual or emotional, upbeat or angry (for instance, note the difference between messages that focus on tobacco control versus those that promote healthy nutrition)
4. The source of the information with specific attention to that source's credibility regarding the issue (e.g., the Minister of Health versus the mother of a sick child); the visual appeal, recognition value, and meaningfulness of the logo to be used
5. The phasing of the messages (i.e., determining how the message should evolve over time or, for instance, in a multiple risk-factor prevention program, defining what specific behavioral or content area should be addressed first and later)

Communication strategies and tactics that make the social idea familiar, acceptable, and desirable to the target audience are the objectives of promotion. Promotion can be accomplished through a marketing mix of any or all of the following:

- *Selling:* Any form of nonpersonal presentation of ideas, goods, or services paid for by an identified sponsor
- *Personal selling:* Any form of paid personal presentation or promotion involving direct face-to-face communication

- *Publicity:* Any form of unpaid nonpersonal presentation of ideas, goods, or services
- *Sales:* Any promotional activity (other than those cited above) that stimulates interest, trial, or purchase of goods or services.

Finally, the distribution of products, services, or materials must be given as much emphasis as the promotion itself, because promising and then failing to come through is a much more disagreeable outcome than never having made an effort in the first place. Distribution factors include whether adequate materials exist; whether sufficient transportation is available to distribute these materials and transport staff, volunteers, and program participants; whether there is an adequate sales force (e.g., trained facilitators) to carry out the program; and whether contingency plans are in place if there is an excessive demand for the products or services.

Selecting channels and developing products. Channels of message delivery include forms of mass and face-to-face or interpersonal communication. Interpersonal communication, central to the human experience, is an integral theme of health promotion. As illness and health have their roots in social existence, the modification or mobilization of interpersonal forces is usually the direct or indirect objective of health promotion programs. Working through natural caregivers, family members, friends, teachers, or clinicians, the effectiveness of our programs can be generalized and maintained.

In spite of its appeal, the use of face-to-to face communication in social marketing programs presents major challenges. Through a pyramiding approach, the effects of communication are presumed to expand through second and even subsequent generations of multipliers, change agents who, after enhancing their own health, attempt to promote similar changes in people with whom they are in regular contact. For example, "Each One Teach One" literacy campaigns in developing countries promoted literacy skills among groups of adult students in diverse communities, with the expectation that these students would, in turn, share this gift with at least one neighbor or relative. Such campaigns have met with only modest success, however. Although the initial wave of learners may be able and personally motivated to learn to read and write or mind their own children's health, this does not necessarily mean they have the skills and motivation necessary to teach. Without additional booster training, monitoring, feedback, and reinforcement, using all available channels of communication and organizational support from the government, the quality of the communication will diminish, volunteers will drop out, and other problems will ensue.

Mass communication is subdivided into print and broadcast media. Print must be actively read or seen, whereas broadcast must be heard or seen. The second primary difference is that print generally can be read (and re-read) at the reader's convenience, but broadcast messages must be attended to when broadcast.

Other differences between print and broadcast include pricing (print costs are based on space used and are generally priced lower; broadcast is based on time and occasionally includes free public service announcement slots), formats available (print generally has more), and locations available (print can be read anywhere). Finally, print is appropriate when longer attention spans are required, whereas broadcast sound bites can reach larger numbers of people for shorter periods of time. Ideally, these two, as well as other channels, are used to complement one another and create an optimal promotional effect (see Table 2.1).

Print media can also be an effective component of communications or at times can stand alone as a health promotion tool. Among print media that emphasize behavior change are comic books (or "photo novels") with a health theme, training manuals, and counseling cards meant to guide a health worker's diagnostic and prescriptive actions. In contrast, pamphlets, brochures, flyers, and posters can help set a community agenda but often emphasize the promotion of a specific event or the agenda once it has been set. An effective distribution approach is to work within organizations and community groups (e.g., schools and places of worship) to make use of their central locations where people can walk by and pick up various print media.

Terms that are commonly used in social marketing, especially with respect to print media, include *primary audience* (those who are exposed to the message in its original presentation), *secondary audience* (those who have a magazine, brochure, or other print piece that was "passed along" to them), and *circulation* (the number of newspapers, magazines, fliers, etc., sold or otherwise distributed to the audience).

The formats of print media are highly varied; program goals, resources, and experience will dictate which are chosen for any given effort. For example, billboards, buttons, banners, flyers, hats, and posters may serve as excellent promotional formats for increasing awareness of a topic. Calendars, height and weight charts, and other self-maintained medical records may serve as specific guides to subsequent behavior. The extra details afforded by the use of flip charts, newsletters, direct mail, and occasionally newspapers are useful for skills training. Finally, stickers, T-shirts, and diplomas can serve as effective rewards for both direct and vicarious behavior change.

Table 2.1 presents the various health communication channels and their advantages and disadvantages (Academy for Educational Development, 1995; Elder et al., 1994).

TABLE 2.1 Advantages and Disadvantages of Major Channels of Communication

Channel	Purposes and Advantages	Disadvantages
Interpersonal	Exploits most common form of human communication and most powerful source of influence	Difficult and time consuming to train and motivate multipliers
	Inexpensive	Difficult to monitor or manage
	Involves the target audience in a participatory process	
	Effective for detail training and reinforcement and for sensitive topics, especially if accompanied by audiovisual or graphic materials	
	Gives credibility to mass media message	
Circulating print	Format allows for extensive detail; good for knowledge/skill acquisition and vicarious learning	Production quality must be attended to
	Involves reader in a factual, detailed rational message	Distribution may be limited or logistically complicated
	News events covered by newspaper result in inexpensive, detailed promotion	Paid advertisements may be expensive
	Magazines and pass-alongs may have long life	Reader may ignore print altogether

	Advantages	Disadvantages
	Explains more complex health issues	Newspaper has short life
	Read at reader's convenience, and may be passed around.	
Display print	May be used as points-of-purchase or otherwise where health-decision behavior occurs	Production and space rental may be expensive
	Certain formats (e.g., billboards) may reach large audience	Not good for knowledge/skill acquisition
	Other formats may provide step-by-step instructions for skill acquisition and behavior change	May be difficult to control and maintain placement
	Good for getting attention/promoting awareness/reinforcement	
Radio	Reaches large audience	Audience attention not assured
	Can use news items and public service announcements (PSAs)	PSA timing may be unattractive
	Good for awareness/recognition reinforcement	Advertisements are expensive
	Various formats allow for specific audience targeting	Difficult to develop "newsworthy" stories

TABLE 2.1 *(continued)*

Channel	Purposes and Advantages	Disadvantages
Television	Visual stimuli make message even more powerful; other advantages similar to those for radio	Even more expensive production and air time than radio
	Provides status to message	PSAs not as available through radio
	Large reach in regions where ownership is common	Difficult to tailor to specific subgroups
		Requires access
Telephone	Inexpensive if implemented through volunteers	Negative public reaction possible
	Especially good for initiating and maintaining behavior change programs	Takes trained change agent if behavioral counseling is conducted
		High rates for no-answers and hang-ups
		Requires access

Learning Theory

The term *learning theory* is most closely connected with B. F. Skinner (1953) and his work in operant psychology (which he referred to as the "experimental analysis of behavior"). Preceding Skinner's extraordinary accomplishments and anticipating some of them were those of John Watson in the United States and Ivan Pavlov in Russia. Albert Bandura (1977b), the person most closely identified with social learning theory, demonstrated how individuals need not personally experience reinforcement, punishment, or other consequences to learn from them. In this book, learning theory is used broadly to refer to research and applications that emphasize direct or vicarious learning through the interaction between behaviors and consequences. This behavior-consequence emphasis distinguishes learning theory from most health communications models (especially communications-persuasion), which primarily focus on modifying behaviors through changing antecedents to them.[1]

Health communication and social marketing techniques are held to be valuable and effective procedures for altering protective or risk-related behavior. Indeed, marketing strategies may be particularly useful in prompting an initial behavior change. However, marketing should not be expected to sustain behavior change, except when the new behavior is reinforced by consequences intrinsic to the task or available in the environmental setting.

Social marketing and applied learning theory (especially contingency management/behavior modification) differ in a variety of other important features. Most health communication campaigns attempt to change cognitive factors such as the consumer's attention, attitude, knowledge, or beliefs. The theoretical assumption underlying these campaigns is that new cognitive processes will lead to informed decisions to change behavior because people's beliefs have changed with respect to the behavior. From a learning theory perspective, the tactics used to change knowledge, attitudes, and beliefs are largely antecedent-oriented educational procedures. In other words, they represent stimuli that set the stage for the occurrence of the behavior through forging antecedent behavior or A-B links. Learning-theory-based procedures, in contrast, emphasize behavior-consequence (B-C) associations or "contingencies."

Behavior modification, or more specifically contingency management, has been defined as "the systematic application of principles derived from learning theory to altering environment behavior relationships in order to strengthen adaptive and weaken maladaptive behaviors" (Elder et al., 1994, p. 128). These behavior-environment relationships that cause and maintain behavior are referred to by

Skinner (e.g., 1953) as contingencies of reinforcement. Hence, contingency management is the application, removal, or discontinuation of consequences in the strengthening or weakening of a behavior. Applying pleasant consequences or removing or discontinuing unpleasant ones will strengthen behaviors through the processes of positive reinforcement, negative reinforcement, or response facilitation. Removing a pleasant consequence, applying an aversive consequence, or discontinuing a pleasant consequence will weaken behaviors. The first two of these latter contingencies are technically referred to as punishment, whereas the latter is referred to as extinction (Elder et al., 1994, pp. 129-131; Sulzer-Azaroff & Mayer, 1991). Although not all six of these contingencies form part of the public health promotion armamentarium, understanding the processes of how behaviors are formed or eliminated is critical to developing campaigns, policies, and other behavior-change interventions.

The HealthCom Project, a child survival effort in over 15 developing countries worldwide, was one of the first to employ learning-theory-based procedures in public health communications campaigns (Academy for Educational Development, 1995). HealthCom identified various criteria for selecting target behaviors, including the health impact of the behavior, its perceptible positive reinforcers, and any punishers or barriers to its performance; the compatibility of the behavior to existing practices, or their similarity; and the ease or complexity of engaging in the behavior in general and specifically at the rate and duration required to alleviate a health problem. Program planners can weight these criteria differently in the design of campaigns, environmental interventions, or policies that promote adaptive and/or weaken unhealthy behavioral alternatives.

Skill Versus Performance Deficits

Health psychology needs to go beyond the establishment of appropriate contingencies to strengthen healthy behaviors or, at times, weaken unhealthy behaviors. Less optimal levels of behavior may result from either a performance or skill deficit. In the former case, contingency management procedures are in order, whereas when skill deficits are present, additional training with appropriate skill-building supervision would be indicated (Graeff, Elder, & Booth, 1993). Alternatively, application of social learning-theory concepts of modeling (vicarious learning through the observation of others), self-efficacy (confidence in a skill or being able to handle a specific situation), and outcome expectations (subjective estimation of the probability that a reinforcer or punisher will follow the performance of a behavior) afford the opportunity for the learning to occur without personal experience of consequences. The individual would need to see other people performing the behavior, develop the necessary confidence about the particular act, and believe that reinforcement will be optimal and/or punishment minimal. According to Bandura (1977a), meeting these criteria should be sufficient to promote behavior change.

For example, how would we know if inadequate service provision by a clinician or other health worker stems from skill deficits or performance deficits? Skill deficits may be inferred when health workers have limited training or even general education, or their training is dated; when poor interaction skills are observed with patients, regardless of how motivated health workers seem to be; or when health workers express low levels of confidence in their abilities to perform even slightly complicated tasks. Performance deficits, on the other hand, may occur when health workers receive little reinforcement for their work or when the rewards they do receive are not really linked with their performance; when they seem unappreciated by their supervisors, peers, or the community they serve; when the expectations that health workers have regarding material and professional status or upward mobility do not match the current reality; or when punishers for and barriers to doing a good job (e.g., no transport, supplies, or cooperation from village leadership) outweigh the job's rewards (Graeff et al., 1993). Health workers are often the primary rather than secondary audience in large-scale behavior-change efforts. With respect to the most appropriate type of reinforcer for health worker performance, research has shown that some expression of gratitude on the part of the community, supplemented by money or work uniforms, should such resources exist, can be extremely effective in motivating and maintaining community service (Reis, Elder, Satoto, Kodyat, & Palmer, 1991).

The single key feature in maintaining effective health worker behavior is providing supervision beyond the period of training. Supervision may occur through a variety of channels, including face-to-face, telephone, or mail. The latter form is the most costly but arguably far more effective. Even if such supervision is infrequent, health workers should expect to be in touch with their supervisors on a regular basis. Not only can health workers receive feedback with respect to how they are performing a clinical skill, but they also get a feeling that "someone cares" about their work.

A similar expression of gratitude from the community being served can complement that from the supervisor. Mass media can be used to vicariously reinforce health workers (or mothers, etc.) or promote expressions of appreciation on the part of the community. Radio spots and other channels can explain to the community the value of good health care and the need to show gratitude for such health

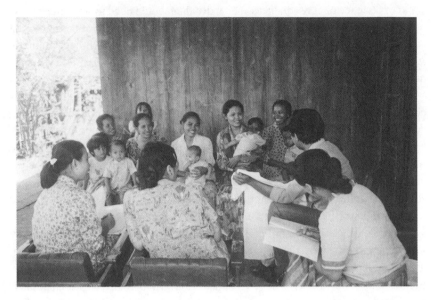

In this group, village mothers help program planners identify appropriate reinforcers for Indonesian health worker volunteers.

care, especially when the providers are volunteers or health workers who are min-imally paid. An example of a radio spot used in central Java, Indonesia, promoting expressions of gratitude among villagers is presented in Table 2.2 (Reis, personal communication, 1989). This combination of health communication and contin-gency management techniques directly addresses performance deficits on the part of health workers and indirectly addresses skill deficits among the people they serve, who need to learn more about expressing their gratitude to the health work-ers.

Health communication and learning-theory-based models provide divergent perspectives on planning and implementing public health behavior-change interventions. Two additional models—media advocacy and community self-control—complement and integrate these primary intervention approaches.

Media Advocacy

Wallack (1990) among others advocates the use of media to advance social change. He points out that although mass media can be an important source of

TABLE 2.2 Modeling and Vicarious Positive Reinforcement Via Radio Spots: Reinforcing Village Health Workers in Indonesia

Intro:	(music)
Mom I:	Well . . . Cempluk looks cheerful, healthy, and alive. She's just recently recovered from diarrhea, hasn't she?
Mom II:	Thanks to Allah, after I kept on giving her drinks and nutritious food, Cempluk seemed well.
Mom I:	Hey . . . how do you know that food and drink should not be stopped for a child who has diarrhea?
Mom II:	From the kader. That's Mother Siti who usually weighs the young kids and gives advice on health.
Mom I:	Well, that kader knows everything, doesn't she?
Mom II:	Yes, right. Since she was trained by the health center, she can give advice on how to keep children really healthy.

health information, they are a primary source of health misinformation as well, and even promote unhealthy lifestyles. Moreover, Wallack asserts that even at their best, the media usually represent health as an individual responsibility rather than as the product of societal forces. Media role models and advertising add to the promotion of instant gratification and the minimization of risks associated with this gratification. Wallack states that because "mass media generally serve to reinforce existing arrangements and not stimulate social change, this perspective on health promotion represents a challenge to public health professionals and the mass media to rethink basic assumptions" (p. 148). Decrying the power of tobacco, alcohol, and other forces of illness in our society, he calls for more creative and aggressive approaches in health promotion's use of the media.

Wallack and Dorfman (1996) suggest a reorientation away from traditional antecedent-oriented health communication approaches toward a methodology that promotes public agenda setting, away from individual and toward societal responsibility for health. Media advocacy maintains a behavior-change focus, only in this case, the behavior of policy makers rather than individual citizens is of interest. Members of the legislative and executive branches of government at all levels are responsible for structuring environments that reinforce healthy behaviors and make unhealthy ones less appealing. Policy makers are unlikely to fund universal child health care, raise taxes on tobacco and alcohol, pass clean indoor-air acts, control gun sales, or promote conservation without pressure from the public to do so. Media advocacy in developing countries must not only confront these same illness industries but also consider economic and other forces that threaten health and the environment. Examples of the latter are the marketing of baby formula and diarrhea treatments, the destruction of rain forests through slash-and-burn agriculture, and the depletion of underwater habitats and fish stocks through dynamite fishing.

Attributing to social marketing a "relatively narrow, reductionist approach," Wallack (1990) notes that appeals to change health behavior in exchange for a reinforcer that is delayed until the distant future will have little success in maintaining behavior change. Media advocacy, thus, integrates the antecedent-oriented techniques of social marketing and health communication with policy changes and other processes that parallel techniques based in learning theory. Media advocacy provides both carrots and sticks to back up the promise of health communication. It shifts the focus of behavior modification from the behavior of ordinary citizens to that of the powerful: politicians, health officials, employers, and others.

Media Advocacy in Action: Promoting Environmentally Friendly Behaviors in Philippine Fisheries

An example of media advocacy comes from a program promoting "environmentally friendly behaviors" (EFBs) in the Philippines. EFBs may fail to occur because a person (a) does not have adequate knowledge or skill with respect to how to protect the environment, (b) there are too many aversive consequences or barriers related to the EFB, or (c) the behavior has insufficient positive consequences (Elder & Douglass, 1996). If a fisherman, for instance, does not know how to build fish cages or a policeman's diligent enforcement of environmental laws is met with indifference on the part of his superiors, we cannot expect these behaviors to persist. In environmental efforts to change EFBs, target behaviors are selected on two general criteria: (a) the impact such behavior will have on protecting the environment and (b) the feasibility of increasing the frequency and prevalence of these behaviors. Within the second criterion are four factors: the availability of positive reinforcement for the behaviors, the complexity of the behaviors, the presence of the behavior among some "early adopters" or in some form or approximation among the population in general, and the material, social, or personal cost or other barriers associated with the behavior. In general, social marketing and contingency management procedures should be adequate to increase the adoption and maintenance of these EFBs.

But a third reason an EFB may not occur is because environmentally unfriendly behaviors (EUBs) have a much greater payoff. Just as a South American farmer may decide to grow cocoa leaves for cocaine instead of far less profitable food crops, illegal loggers and fishermen using dynamite and cyanide are also making logical, profit-centered decisions.

When, then, should EUBs be targeted? Generally, environmental communication programs emphasize positive behaviors over disruptive ones, such as "disposing of garbage in proper receptacles" rather than "not throwing garbage in the street," planting trees instead of not cutting them down, and enforcing the law rather than not letting violators go free. At times, however, a behavior-change strategy will have to include sticks as well as carrots. Policy is a tool for behavior change and, thus, must be understood as something decided on through representative government for the common good. The common good may be translated into individual benefits and media messages: Sustainable logging results in long-term profit, tree planting slows erosion, protection of reefs promotes tourism, and the creation of fish sanctuaries increases the catch.

Environmental policy may not always contain sufficient positive reinforcers to actually stop an EUB, especially when this behavior is highly profitable. In such cases, the government can pass legislation that adds incentives to the naturally occurring ones. For example, laws may specify a grace period for legal sales of illicitly gained inventories, tax incentives for replanting forests, and favorable licensing for other EFBs.

But good laws must also specify any punishments needed to stop violators. Criminal prosecution of illegal logging, tax evasion, and fencing; civil litigation for environmental injury; and administrative sanctions such as cancellation of licenses are examples of sanctions that may be necessary counterparts to incentives for obeying the law. Environmental communication, then, takes on a media advocacy role, seeking to educate the public about the law through information and publicity given to cases of its violation and the consequences of that violation. Raids of illegal lumber inventories, arrests for violating fish sanctuaries, and chronic failure to enforce existing laws may all make for good news articles and deter other potential EUBs (if doing so does not put the reporter at risk).

Destruction of marine species and habitat is particularly hard to control. For example, the use of dynamite to kill fish for sale and consumption has been used for 40 years in or near the world's tropical coral reefs. Nevertheless, policies and the media advocacy that supports them do serve a role in containing EUBs. An example of such advocacy was a newspaper article that described an arrest for the catch and slaughter of a rare dolphin near Tabilaron City, Philippines. The record noted the names of the seven men involved, as well as the name of the boat and its owner, thereby not only magnifying their notoriety but also sending a message to other potential violators. In terms of positive reinforcement, the name of the arresting maritime policeman was also noted, as was the fact that these violators were turned in by a group of students on a picnic. This latter mention directly reinforced average citizens for doing their civic duty and provided an opportunity for vicarious learning among others who might be inclined to imitate them in the future.

Criteria for selecting EUBs parallel those for selecting EFBs, with some additional twists. These criteria, again, are based on (a) how adverse the EUB's impact is and (b) the feasibility of doing something about it. Within the feasibility criterion, the following are considered: the cost of no longer engaging in the behavior, the presence of an EFB as a feasible substitute, the availability of policy-based sanctions to reduce the behavior, and/or the safety of the change agent (for example, community residents who report fishing violations). Should these criteria be assessed favorably, EUBs could be targeted along with EFBs in an overall national strategy.

In developing media advocacy interventions, we may consider matching individuals and even entire communities to a "stage of change" (Prochaska & DiClemente, 1983) with respect to environmental protection as well as whether EUBs or EFBs are being targeted. Communities that are pre-contemplators, displaying few if any EFBs, might be targeted with media surrounding the development and enforcement of policy that offers incentives to discontinue the EUB and sanctions should the EUB persist. Complementing this strategy would be unfavorable media coverage of people performing EUBs.

In the case of an absence of EFBs, TV, radio, and other channels might dramatize a potential catastrophe if actions are not taken to protect the environment, ending with a message of hope; such messages might move these communities toward contemplation or action stages. If model ordinances for environmental protection are provided, local governments might find their own ordinance development easier.

For communities already contemplating taking action, media spots that highlight potential reinforcement for EFBs can document "early adopter" actions and reinforcement they receive for these actions. For example, after several years of mangrove conservation, communities are rewarded not only by more trees but also by more fish and birds. Providing local governments with environmental resource identification can also be helpful when they seek assistance in developing their own action plans.

In the early stage of initiating an EFB, public recognition from the media, governmental agencies, places of worship, and NGOs can be effective in maintaining the effort. A regional or national hotline available for answering questions from government officials contributes to better policy enactment and enforcement. These efforts may eventually be complemented by friendly competitions, such as a tree-planting contest, with the winning municipality receiving a letter of commendation from a well-known official.

Once EFBs are initiated, sustaining them becomes the major challenge. Licensing, taxes, or other incentives; media pieces highlighting successes and positive environmental impact of long-term EFBs; and even recruitment of early adopters to advocacy roles can all be effective in sustaining EFBs. Reaching out to promote EFBs among neighbors, colleagues, and other organizations are ways in which media advocacy roles can operate on a smaller scale.

By developing communication oriented toward specific stages of behavior change, we can optimize both the effectiveness and efficiency of the commuication. Expensive television campaigns featuring environmental calamity would not be advisable if the bulk of the audience is already embarking on EFBs. Conversely, public recognition of early adopters would be inappropriate if people engaging in EUBs are proceeding to destroy the environment with impunity.

An example of specific media advocacy activities supporting an overall effort is found in a Cebu City, Philippines, magazine called *The Freeman.* The cover story, "The Miracle That Is Madridlejos" (a municipality on the island of Cebu), lists substantial improvements in this municipality in the first year of a new mayor's term. The article noted that

> Madridlejos is undertaking its own environmental protection through strengthened anti-illegal fishing campaigns, tree planting and replanting of its mangos. The town now has a nursery to back up the tree-planting program despite legal threats due to personal interests of some local politicians. The administration has caught more illegal fishers in one year than all the previous administrations in the past. Due to the special efforts of the new leader of the (municipality) this program is effective.

Thus, this article reinforces the new mayor and other governmental officials for their progressive actions and again sets the stage for similar actions by other communities with access to the publication.

Community Self-Control

International public health initiatives via health communications, learning theory, and media advocacy all offer approaches to broad-based behavior change potentially sufficient to realize a public health or other large-scale impact. However, these and other public health models are predicated on the assumption of *control:* how to change and control behaviors and the diseases to which they lead (Duhl, 1986, p. 17). But Banerji (1999) cautioned,

> By their very nature, international initiatives cannot promote community self-reliance . . . these programs are the very antitheses of the Alma Ata Declaration . . . which envisaged involving the community in the identification of its health needs and priorities as well as in the implementation and management of the various health and related programmes. (p. 240)

Even if initial efforts create change, maintenance of such change may still require intensive efforts on a community-by-community basis. The final element of our intervention model is the development of community self-control, which on a smaller scale may be applied to antecedent, behavior change, or consequence aspects of behavioral interventions (see Figure 2.1).

Vertical programs that establish primary care systems and promote health often overlook the individual parent or health worker whose experience is based not only on socioeconomic realities but also on generations of tradition and the norms of the community. Even when vertical programs are effective, their effect may not be sustainable, as success will lead to a loss of political and financial support for the programs (Gubler, 1989). Psychologist Frederick Kanfer (1975) asserts that for individual behavior change to be effective, self-control must be achieved through mechanisms of self-monitoring, setting achievable goals, experimenting with the behavior change, and conducting self-evaluation and self-reinforcement.

The Healthy Community movement places less emphasis on the control of disease and more on the process of change and the ultimate consequences of that process (U.S. Department of Health and Human Services, 1998). Meant to go beyond the resolution of just a simple problem, the Healthy Community process is meant to inspire action, draw in more participants, provide them with a common purpose, and ensure a sustained commitment (Ashton, 1992). Roland Bunch (1982) outlined a community empowerment approach for developing countries to achieve effective and responsible development that incorporates processes parallel to those outlined by Kanfer (1975). Bunch's approach focuses on small groups or small communities and serves as a model not only for agriculture (his primary

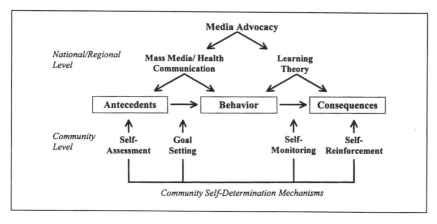

Figure 2.1. An integrated model for public health behavior change.

focus) but also for health and other sectors. Indeed, simply establishing the sense of empowerment could result in one group being able to address needs across a variety of sectors.

First, Bunch's community-intervention approach holds that community improvements can only be accomplished in the context of progress toward broader human goals: meeting the basic necessities of life including adequate food, clothing, shelter, and education; respecting the sociopolitical rights of the target population; encouraging individuals to act in a community spirit; and interacting with religious organizations in areas where religion is a crucial element of a community. The primary theme of his approach is to avoid paternalism, no matter how well-meaning it is. If others accomplish change for individuals, they will have little motivation to do it themselves.

However, sustained efforts for improving heath practices will only occur if there are recognizable successes.[2] Therefore, Bunch (1982) insists that initial targets must be achievable and accomplished with technology that is affordable and available. Health workers' and parents' skills must be gradually shaped over time, rather than through criteria that are set too high to be achieved.

The amount of participation in a community program will depend on the enthusiasm that is created through setting appropriate, achievable goals, as well as other factors:

- Initiating behavior change at a small and simple level involving only early adopter health workers and parents who are initially enthusiastic about it
- Choosing change agents carefully

- Emphasizing those who understand the culture and are willing to keep a low profile in the overall work
- Planning for a phasing out of any outside change agents from the beginning of the program (although this can be done on a gradual basis)
- Teaching health workers and other change agents to conduct small-scale trials rather than trying to convert an entire community at once
- Downplaying the budgetary aspects of a temporary program so as not to raise expectations regarding potential handouts
- Incorporating the community's own health priorities into goals and objectives for the health program, which not only will build trust but also will promote the sustainability of the effort (Perry et al., 1999)
- Trying not to meet all of the people's needs but only to accomplish specific things related to the program
- Constantly monitoring the participation in the program by the entire village

Pre-intervention criteria. Before a program can begin, several criteria must be met. First, primary care and behavior-change technology must be available to respond to health needs in the local area. Second, necessary supplies and equipment for applying this technology must be attainable. Finally, people in the village must really want to benefit from health improvements. Other factors that are also important, although not quite as critical as the previous ones, include the willingness and ability of local people to cooperate and work together; their willingness to work voluntarily for the community's good; attitudes such as honesty, trust, inquisitiveness, and willingness to work hard; and the presence of governmental or other local institutions or of other programs that have succeeded. Hence, needs and resources assessments should be conducted to look not only at health but also at economic, social, political, religious, and cultural realities. Objective readings on these factors will help the change agent to identify the village or groups that will start the program.

Community self-control processes. Once an area is selected for the program, the planning process begins, with village participation as part and parcel of this process. However, if areas are selected carefully, participation should be forthcoming, at least initially. Directly parallel to Kanfer's (1975) individual self-control model, Bunch's (1982) planning process consists of five basic steps:

1. Gathering information
2. Establishing goals and objectives
3. Developing a work plan
4. Preparing the budget
5. Monitoring

Information gathering will occur with respect to many of the same factors discussed above. In many cases, however, the community participants themselves should be doing the information gathering. The data gathered during this phase will then inform the goals and objectives that are established. Goal establishment should be done in a consensus fashion, much in the same way that individuals attempting behavior change negotiate a contingency contract with a professional. However, in community goal-setting, some individual participants may actually object to the ultimate goals selected. A skillful change agent will know how to respond to these objections and still work toward overall consensus and satisfaction with the program.

Specific objectives should be stated in terms of benefits to the participants. For example, an objective might be that through the regular use of impregnated mosquito nets in at least 50% of the homes in the village, the village will witness a 10% overall reduction in malaria-related deaths, while adults in each household adopting this strategy will enjoy 5 fewer days per year of work lost due to illness. Goals and objectives should be established with respect to what problems the villagers see as most pressing, balanced by which ones are the most resolvable. Finally, constant monitoring of a program's activities is essential to maintain a continuing flow of feedback for purposes of self-correction or reinforcement.

Selecting early adopters and target behaviors. Once goals and objectives are established, the intervention procedure may begin. For example, villagers may decide that water quality and safety need to be tackled. The change agent will work with them to identify the most appropriate technology (e.g., latrines, sand filters for water purification) and target behaviors (e.g., building, using, and maintaining the latrines or filters) for accomplishing this (Morales, 1999). Once this technology is identified, however, the program should be launched with only a small number of early adopters. According to Rogers (1983), certain individuals in a community often experiment with and adopt technological and behavioral innovations; other "late adopters" see them as trend setters. These innovators are often imitated by others through the process of vicarious learning (or in their terms, the *diffusion of innovations*), assuming, of course, that their innovation has met with success. Once success is achieved with this smaller group of early adopters, expansion to large populations will prove much easier.

According to Bunch (1982), change agents "can aim at either teaching one idea to hundreds of people or hundreds of ideas to one person" (p. 84). In other words, technology must be limited if it aims for widespread adoption. From a psychological perspective, the extra effort necessitated in building the self-efficacy of individual health workers or parents would severely limit the number of people who could be reached. Thus, the change agent must decide whether to promote oral rehydration therapy, immunizations, cleaner water other environmental modifications, vitamin A consumption, and so forth. However, not all of these advances should be promoted concurrently. The change agent should aim for a critical mass of individuals to adopt a single or limited number of changes to make a large-scale impact.

How, then, should technologies and target behaviors be chosen? General criteria for selection of appropriate technologies are that the target audience recognizes them as successful and that they deal with factors that most affect health, result in a benefit to the poor, are widely marketable, and are widely applicable. For technologies to be recognized by all as being successful, they must meet a perceived need, appear to be financially manageable, bring success relatively quickly, and fit local practices. Finally, it must be possible to communicate the technology efficiently, with a minimum of labor-intensive on-site supervision visits and a fairly simple teaching strategy.

Behavioral trials and vicarious learning. Before the change agent promotes widespread adoption of a new behavior or technology (e.g., mixing and administering oral rehydration solutions, eliminating mosquito-breeding sites), individual early adopters should be recruited and encouraged to experiment with it. These innovators can then experience for themselves how much effort is required and what costs are incurred, as well as what benefits are produced. Their health or that of their children, then, will serve as a feedback mechanism for adjusting their behavior or for reinforcing it and promoting vicarious learning to others. Change agents are required to do less "hands-on" work in promoting the technology to additional villagers, as they can give them a tour of the experimental plot and show what possibilities exist. To multiply this effect, the change agent can go through a standard process of behavioral skills development (telling—showing—practicing—giving feedback—reinforcing) by having the successful early adopter model the new behavior and teach it to others. Learning-theory-based procedures in the form of written behavioral contracts developed with the early adopters may increase their commitment to adopting the new practice and (should it be successful) teaching it to many of their neighbors. Mass media can be used to back up the face-to-face communication as well.

Is community self-control always best? Reiter and Gubler (1997) compare and contrast two national experiences in mosquito control for dengue-fever prevention (see Chapter 5). In Singapore, beginning in the 1960s, educational campaigns promoted the elimination of mosquito-infested containers. Government inspectors made frequent visits to homes to reinforce the message and inspect for mosquito larvae. Residents of homes positive for larvae were subject to fines. In Cuba, a campaign was launched in 1981 via rigorous house-to-house inspections with larvicides put in nondisposable containers and the destruction of disposable ones. This was backed by malathion spraying from planes and vehicles.

Both of these vertical programs are among the most successful in the history of dengue control. However, dengue incidence rose somewhat again in Singapore, as the inspections came to be seen as intrusive and hence became unpopular. Cuba currently relies far more on community control to sustain its initial vertical success. Generalizing from these experiences is difficult: Both Cuba and Singapore have highly disciplined populations in terms of accepting public health interventions, and both are small island nations. But one can conclude that national and international efforts are often, by necessity, vertical in nature at the outset but can only realize long-term success as control devolves to the community level.

SUMMARY

Many psychosocial theories current in health psychology and health education have limited applicability to developing-country populations and health issues, where more traditional cultures and subordination of individual to community identity prevail. Four general theories or models of behavior change are relatively more practical with respect to developing health promotion programs in the developing-country context:

1. Health communications and social marketing, based in the communications-persuasion model, which focuses on specific steps: exposure to, understanding of, and response to health messages

2. Learning theory, especially as represented by operant psychology and social learning theory, with its emphasis on behavior-consequence relationships that may either sustain maladaptive or promote health behavior

3. Media advocacy, which, like health communications, emphasizes mass media and similar applied learning theory; it looks at behavior-consequence relationships, only this time the behavior of decision makers rather than typical consumers

4. Community self-control, linking antecedent, behavior change, and consequence-based interventions together on a local basis, with representative community residents selecting target behaviors and specific tools for achieving change

FURTHER READING

Bandura, A. (1977). *Social learning theory.* Englewood Cliffs NJ: Prentice Hall.

Glanz, K., Lewis, F., & Rimer, B. (1997). *Health behavior and health education: Theory, research, and practice* (2nd ed.). San Francisco: Jossey-Bass.

Rogers, E. M. (1983). *Diffusion of innovations.* New York: Free Press.

Siegel, M., & Doner, L. (1998). *Marketing public health: Strategies to promote social change.* Gaithersburg, MD: Aspen.

Skinner, B. F. (1953). *Science and human behavior.* New York: Macmillan.

Sulzer-Azaroff, B., & Mayer, G. R. (1991). *Behavior analysis for lasting change.* Fort Worth, TX: Harcourt Brace.

▓ Notes

1. In a broader sense, however, effective health communication, such as the family planning campaign described on pages 64-67, emphasizes both antecedent-behavior and behavior-consequence relationships.

2. Which returns to the contradictions between the CBIO epidemiologically based approach to identifying those at highest risk suggested by Perry and colleagues (1999) and the population "upstream" emphasis espoused by McKinlay and Marceau (1999, 2000). Communities may be far more likely to understand basic epidemiological concepts and approve of prioritizing those at highest risk in terms of resource allocation and program development. Yet, as McKinlay and Marceau (1999) note, small and even imperceptible improvements in everyone's health will yield greater overall gains for a society than very perceptible improvements in the health of a minority. Examining an entire population curve and attempting a shift in the entire population, even when individual efforts may not have a high probability of paying off, may prove an abstract and unpopular concept. Yet, McKinlay and Marceau (2000) deride government-sponsored public health in the pluralist society as a "weather vane, blown in whatever direction the public dictates" (p. 30), seeming to imply that only socially enlightened public health experts should set policy. This discussion will be revisited in Chapter 8.

3

Nutrition

The nutritional condition of the human population will largely dictate the health of that population. In turn, this nutritional condition is heavily influenced by various social, cultural, and ecological factors (Brown & Solomon, 1991). The nutritional status of populations in developing countries generally stems from deficiency rather than excess, closely associated with other indicators of poverty. These populations are heavily reliant on plant sources of nutrients rather than animal sources, and they are easily affected by adverse environmental conditions, which in turn contribute to a high prevalence of infectious diseases. Although impoverished communities in industrialized countries may experience aspects of undernutrition as well, it is often in combination with some nutritional excess.

Vast proportions of developing-country populations are threatened by malnutrition, including deficiencies in protein, calories, and other nutrients. It is estimated that 175 million people (mostly children) are malnourished worldwide, with nearly two thirds of these in Asia (Black, 1999). About 1.2 billion people consume fewer daily calories than would be recommended (Gardner & Halweil, 2000).

Nutritional deficiencies may be classified in terms of specific nutrient categories or specific disease syndromes related to that deficiency. For instance, one can alternately refer to iron deficiency, anemia, or nutritional problems of demographic subgroups affected by iron deficiency (Brown & Solomon, 1991, p. 298). Specific nutrient deficiencies that are fairly common in developing countries include protein-energy malnutrition (PEM), nutritional anemia; and vitamin A, iron, and iodine deficiency. Three major high-risk population subgroups affected by these and other diseases are newborns, children under 5 years old, and women of reproductive age. Breast-fed newborns are largely protected from most major nutrient deficiencies, even if their mothers are malnourished. Nevertheless, newborns may suffer from iodine deficiency and to some extent from PEM, as well.

Young children are at high risk for many forms of malnutrition, especially if they are ill from diarrhea-related disease (see Chapter 5). "Under fives" may suffer from PEM, iron deficiency/anemia, vitamin A deficiency, and to a lesser extent, iodine deficiency, riboflavin deficiency, or zinc deficiency. Finally, young mothers and other women of reproductive age may be vulnerable to anemia and iodine deficiency and also may be affected by PEM and vitamin A deficiency (Brown & Solomon, 1991).

PEM in young children may result either in low height-for-age (stunting) or low weight-for-height (wasting). Weight-for-age is often used as the primary indicator, given the simplicity of its measurement; however, the distinction between stunting and wasting may be important. Stunting may result from intrauterine growth retardation, largely due to maternal malnutrition before and during pregnancy. Stunting or wasting may result from inadequate dietary intakes among newborn and under-five children, as well as from postnatal infections. Risk factors for PEM include poverty, multiparity, and even gender of the child (Brown & Solomon, 1991). Postnatal growth retardation generally occurs between 6 and 24 months of age. Globally, South Asia leads the world in low weight for age, followed by Southeast Asia, Equatorial Africa, North Africa, the Middle East, Central America, and South America.

Robert Black (1999) asserts that children who are as little as one standard deviation below the mean for weight and height have an increased risk of disease and death. Malnutrition is inextricably linked to frequent infections, which in turn result in catabolism, anorexia, malabsorption, and reduced intake (thus further accelerating the malnutrition). For this reason, children in developing countries who lose weight seldom recover.

Unfortunately, children are at peak risk at the same time that nutritional demands are highest for women of reproductive age: during pregnancy and lactation. As a result, low birth weight is found among 30% of South Asian infants and between 10% and 20% of those in Africa and Central America (World Bank, 1997). PEM has severe behavioral as well as physical consequences, leading to reductions in final body size and muscle mass, a decrease in physical activity, lower work capacity, and immunosuppression (Brown & Solomon, 1991).

Breast-Feeding

Breast milk is the gold standard of all infant foods. Breast milk includes lactose as its predominant carbohydrate, with lactose and fat providing 90% of the calories contained in breast milk. Breast-feeding results in enhanced protection against many infectious diseases, while minimizing the infant's exposure to environmental pathogens. Breast milk can even play a curative role, especially in the case of diarrheal disease. Overall, mortality rates among infants in developing countries are three to five times higher in formula-fed than in breast-fed infants (Howard & Weitzman, 1992). Even in developed countries, breast-feeding results in a re-

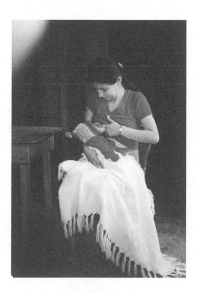

Breast milk is the gold standard of all infant foods.

duced incidence of gastroenteritis, urinary tract infections, ear infections, eczema, and Sudden Infant Death Syndrome (SIDS).

Breast-feeding promotes bonding and perhaps even higher intelligence levels. Breast-feeding mothers are less likely to develop breast and ovarian cancer before menopause or hip fractures in old age (Barrowclough, 1997).

The promotion of breast-feeding through social services programs such as the supplemental nutrition program for women, infants, and children (WIC) can be extremely cost effective. For example, in a study of the WIC program conducted by Montgomery and Splett (1997), breast-feeding saved between $160 and $478 per infant over the course of 6 months, especially through a reduced reliance not only on powder formula but also on pharmacy products in general.

Thus the effects of breast-feeding are entirely salutary, especially with respect to preventing malnutrition and strengthening the baby to fight off disease or recover from an illness. For instance, a study of Nigerian children with diarrhea and dysentery (Meremikwu, Asindi, & Antia-Obong, 1997) showed that the prevalence of diarrhea among breast-fed children was significantly lower. Breast-fed children were nearly five times less likely to have persistent diarrhea, whereas 7.4% of nonbreast-fed and only 5.8% of breast-fed children showed evidence of dysentery (a result approaching but not reaching statistical significance). In this study, 35.9% of breast-fed compared to 49.6% of nonbreast-fed babies were at least somewhat underweight.

Labeled the "nutrition minimum package," breast-feeding plays a pivotal role in overall efforts to promote child health through changing nutritional behaviors (Lutter et al., 1997). The health and nutrition-related behaviors that comprise the bulk of the package include (a) exclusive breast-feeding for 6 months; (b) appropriate complementary feedings starting at 6 months in addition to breast-feeding, which should last at least 24 months total; (c) adequate vitamin A intake for women, infants, and young children; (d) appropriate nutritional management during and after illness; (e) iron and folate supplements taken by all pregnant women; and (f) regular use of iodized salt by all families.

The United Nations International Children's Education Fund (UNICEF) estimates that 1 million infant lives could be saved each year through the successful promotion of exclusive breast-feeding. Studies indicate that babies who are exclusively bottle-fed have about five times the mortality risk of those who are breast-fed, although there is some dispute as to whether exclusive breast-feeding is truly superior to predominant breast-feeding (Victora et al., 1998). Other health problems associated with bottle-feeding include formulas mixed with diluted and contaminated water, improper cleansing of equipment, and spoilage. Conversely, there are many direct benefits of breast-feeding, which clearly point to the need to promote this action. These include the fact that using human milk saves the family money and may even save a nation's resources by reducing the reliance on imported infant formula. Breast-feeding is an ideal food, in terms of quality and quantity, for the infant; infants are protected from infections via breast-feeding; and breast-feeding may reduce the risk of additional pregnancies (Wilmoth & Elder, 1995). Unfortunately, prenatal HIV transmission may actually take place through the ingestion of breast milk as well as through gestation, labor, and delivery (Sharma & Willingham, 1997). However, the benefits of breast-feeding usually substantially outweigh the potential risk of HIV transmission through breast-feeding, except in areas where the prevalence of HIV infection is extremely high or for some reason the difference in mortality between breast-fed and bottle-fed babies is very low.

Growth Monitoring

Growth monitoring in early childhood is used to promote and sustain good health and growth in children under 5 (and especially under 2) and to detect early growth failure due to a variety of causes, including inadequate diets, infections, maternal practices, or a combination of these factors. Growth monitoring is, therefore, more than a simple measurement of growth itself, which would be useful only as data gathering without interpretation and feedback. Its sentinel role is crucial, given that children who lose substantial weight are not likely to gain it back (Black, 1999). Even more than breast-feeding, promotion of growth monitoring relies on the communication and technical skills of the primary health care worker.

Growth monitoring has been promoted for decades and has been a central theme in underdeveloped areas of the world where essential protein and energy are scarce (Morely, 1968). Seemingly a simple procedure, growth-monitoring systems can unravel when health workers receive poor training or equipment is costly or unreliable, when excessively large numbers of children need to be served, and when services for interpretation of growth problems and referrals for inadequate growth are unavailable or inadequate (Jelliffe & Jelliffe, 1990).

Jelliffe and Jelliffe (1990) outlined the critical behavioral issues related to the use of growth monitoring in underdeveloped countries in their book *Growth Monitoring and Promotion in Young Children*. They listed five primary health-worker responsibilities and skill areas for implementing a growth monitoring system, including (a) motivating mothers to bring their children into the clinic or place of service to be monitored, (b) measuring weight accurately, (c) recording weight accurately on graphs or charts, (d) interpreting the child's condition from the growth achieved, and (e) taking appropriate action with respect to the child's growth process, especially if this action involves remediation for inadequate growth. According to these authors, however, growth-monitoring systems break down with maturity of the child, when nutritional status itself rather than growth is emphasized, when no feedback is given to the mothers about the child's growth progress, when services rendered are not individualized to the particular mother-child pair and their own reality, when the belief that growth monitoring and promotion is simple and therefore easy, and when there is lack of community involvement.

Two essential tools are required for promoting growth monitoring: a weighing scale or some other form of measurement of weight and a chart, graph, or other method of recording that weight. The selection of the appropriate instrument will depend on a variety of factors such as cost, the literacy and experience of health workers providing the services, the ease of use, and the volume of children who can be measured with a given instrument (Jelliffe & Jelliffe, 1990, p. 9). The choice between balance beam and spring scales, for example, can be a fairly complicated one. The fundamental design of the instrument; the resources required for its maintenance, safety, and durability; its portability; its acceptability both to the operator and the mother; its potential for error, as well as the associated potential for operator error; and its cost and complexity are all factors related to an appropriate choice. (Some of these same issues would apply to the measurement of height; however, height itself is rarely a part of the overall growth measurement strategy in underdeveloped countries.)

The actual recording of the weight is the next important factor to consider in developing a growth-monitoring and promotion system. Only through the recording of serial weights, preferably through at least three consecutive weigh-ins at appropriate intervals, can a line slope be calculated and an appropriate judgment be made as to whether a child is experiencing adequate growth. The first year of the child's life should show evidence of relatively steep increases in weight. To the degree that this weight gain flattens out, the health worker must begin to inquire why no growth is being achieved. Actual deceleration in the growth line after two or three measures is a clear sign of a dangerous situation, to which the health workers must respond with extra care and/or a referral. Growth charts often have lines indicating upper and lower bounds of appropriate weight for a child's age. This allows the health worker and mother to place the child's progress in a statistically based context. However, multiple lines showing different percentiles of growth, with the addition of coloring to show multiple specific categories of *very good, good, adequate, poor,* or *very poor* growth, may end up confusing both the mother and health worker. Other information may be included on the growth-monitoring card, as well, including records of other well-baby procedures (especially immunizations) and written and visual information on prescribed health-behavior issues such as promoting green leafy vegetables in a diet. The most appropriate card format is one that presents the strongest educational tool for the mother: being comprehensible, alerting her to potential danger signs, and pointing out health-promoting measures that she can take both in conjunction with the health services provided and on her own as a homemaker.

Growth-monitoring weigh-ins are often provided on a monthly basis, in conjunction with other services, such as immunization and health education talks and dispensing of food supplements, packaged or rehydration salts, and other products. Weigh-ins should be monthly for 3 years and are especially important during this first year. However, as a practical matter, children should be weighed every time they visit a health post.

When the mother visits the health post, inquiries can be made about the child's birth weight, the size of the parents (to give a context of the expected growth for the child), the breast-feeding and weaning history of the child, and the signs and symptoms of any infections. When the child is at the clinic for the first weighing, the health worker has little information to go on except actual weight. Therefore, cards with lines indicating normal weight ranges are highly useful in guiding the health worker's behavior, at least on this initial basis. Children who weigh in well below the mean should be referred for further diagnostic procedures, especially if they have done so for a second consecutive visit. Weights that are persistently below the mean but above the lower line limit should at least elicit an inquiry to determine what the problem may be. Children who are at or above the normal range and do not evidence edema are probably healthy; their mothers should be encouraged to continue keeping immunizations up-to-date and to continue appropriate breast-feeding and/or weaning. They should be reminded of their next visit date and the importance of coming back for that appointment.

There are three primary causes of unsatisfactory growth (Jelliffe & Jelliffe, 1990, p. 48). The most likely culprit would be deficient diet, translated as inadequate breast-feeding or, for an older child, inadequate consumption of protein and calories due to insufficient food available to the family or to maldistribution of the food available within the household. Infections also lead to inadequate growth, especially diarrhea or acute respiratory infections (Black, 1999). Finally, poor child care may result at least indirectly in inadequate growth, as the mother may not have the knowledge or time available (especially in the case of large families) to take care of her youngest child.

When inadequate growth does occur, health workers can consider a variety of tactics. Specific and realistic advice on how to improve the child's diet, as well as that of the mother, may be given. The mother may be taught how to manage some infections, especially through the use of oral rehydration in response to diarrhea. The mother should be encouraged to come back for more frequent observation or if the child is severely ill, the pair should be referred to a better equipped health unit. In all cases, mothers should be positively reinforced for having accomplished any of their necessary child care activities, and they should be encouraged to modify care when needed without being criticized for shortcomings (Jelliffe & Jelliffe, 1990, p. 56). For a sick child, weekly weigh-ins may actually be indicated until the child's growth is back on the right track.

Weight charts, in most cases, are designed to be retained by the mother. However, such home-based records should be duplicated in a centrally held chart, as mothers may lose the card or may forget to bring it back for the next clinic appointment. Maintaining personal records can be a helpful adjunct to health education efforts, especially if the cards are well designed and appropriate for the mother not only to review herself but also to share with the father and other adults who may be involved in the child's care.

Nutritional Interventions

The International Fight Against Formula Feeding

Breast-feeding is a natural practice, universal across time and species. However, mass urbanization of populations throughout the world, as well as continued poverty and low levels of education in these urbanizing populations, has resulted in alarming declines in breast-feeding rates. Low rates of breast-feeding are not directly attributable to women entering the workforce; however, a return to work following childbirth is associated with earlier weaning (Visness & Kennedy, 1997). Aggressive marketing of infant formula, which began in the late 1940s, as well as the passive compliance of health care workers with this marketing push, accelerated the trend toward formula feeding (Wilmoth & Elder, 1995).

Although their own corporations were largely responsible for the worldwide shift from breast- to formula feeding in the first half of the 20th century (Wilmoth & Elder, 1995), industrialized countries in some ways compensated for the unhealthy shift toward bottle feeding through overall improved nutrition and sanitation. Such was not the case in underdeveloped countries, however, where an estimated 1 million children died each year because they were not breast-fed (Elder, et al., 1994). Nevertheless, Nestlé, Borden, and other multinational companies expanded aggressively into international markets, with cynical yet imaginative broadcast, print, and display advertising.

In 1972, the United Nations finally began pressuring the formula industry to tone down its marketing, while a Swiss social action group began domestic and international agitation against the practices of the Swiss-based Nestlé, using techniques that anticipated media advocacy (Chapter 2). In 1977, a coalition of U.S. groups launched the Nestlé boycott.

Although joined by American and many international groups, the boycott was resisted by Nestlé and its supporters in the U.S. government and elsewhere. This resistance further strengthened the resolve of the grassroots organizations involved and stimulated an increasingly broader economic offensive. Nestlé slowly began to modify its marketing practices. Finally, in 1984, the company agreed to limit promotional gift-giving, revise product labels in accord with international code, and work within a strict definition of which infants could be given free formula samples (Elder et al., 1994, pp. 333-334).

Other Interventions to Promote Breast-Feeding

Standard efforts to promote breast-feeding emphasize the behavior not only of the mother but also of the health worker, whose influence during the postpartum period is crucial. La Leche League, Wellstart, and other governmental and nongovernmental programs have developed a variety of print materials and interpersonal communication supplements to highlight the benefits of breast-feeding to these two target audiences (e.g., Joesoeff, Annest, & Utomo, 1989; Matulessy, 1988). Mass media-related efforts to support this largely interpersonal communication approach have two distinct purposes: to promote breast-feeding directly while reducing the appeal of formula by advertising bans (e.g., Baer, 1981; Biddulph, 1981).

Contingency Management in the Philippines

Guthrie, Guthrie, Fernandez, and Estrera (1982) used positive reinforcement to promote improved feeding patterns among young mothers. These mothers were reinforced for maintaining breast-feeding until their children were 12 to 15 months old, supplementing breast milk with solid foods beginning about the fourth month, planting green leafy garden vegetables near the home, returning to the health center each month for weight gain ("well baby") checks, and actually achieving weight gain in their children as verified through these checks. Mothers received reward coupons used for lottery drawings every 3 months, with prizes being sacks of corn or rice provided by the government. Three villages were studied, randomly assigned to either lottery alone, reinforcement with the use of a Polaroid photograph of the mother and baby, or a control condition with only standard health education and weight monitoring. Children from the ages of 12 months to 30 months in the special reinforcement conditions evidenced substantial weight gain and other health advantages. The authors caution against the use of the food-based lottery intervention component, however, as such foodstuffs may not be adequately available or may send confusing signals in a nutritional health program. They suggested that the Polaroid photo as a reinforcer was both cost-effective and adequate.

Community Self-Control in Indonesia

Indonesia promotes the use of aggregate community weight-gain information. Volunteer health workers compile individual growth information and make composite bar graphs for the entire community. The graphs represent the number of children under 3 years old in the community, the number registered with the health clinic and who have a growth card, the total number of children weighed each month, and the total number of those who gained weight during that same time period. These graphs give easily understood feedback on how well the community's children are doing in terms of participation in the clinic program and weight gain, as ideally all bars should be at the same height. If there is a fall-off from the former to the latter categories, program planners and health workers can take corrective action (CHANGE Project, 1999).

Health Communication and Social Marketing in West Africa

Burkina Faso. Parlato and Seidel (1998) presented descriptions of three large-scale nutritional interventions using health communications (and to a lesser extent, contingency management) in West Africa. In a study done in Burkina Faso, an intensive effort was conducted to educate parents about specific actions that would improve their children's nutritional status, beginning with the mother's diet during pregnancy. At the same time, the program sought to promote the skills of health workers providing critical services to these mothers. The objectives of this effort were to improve the diet of pregnant and lactating women; promote exclusive breast-feeding for up to 6 months; ensure that children ate other nutritious foods if they were age-appropriate (especially during bouts of diarrhea); and encourage prenatal visits, growth monitoring, and nutritional health education sessions at health centers. Behavioral targets included eating more food during pregnancy and lactation, including milk, fruit, vegetables, meat, cereals, peanuts, and beans; attending at least three prenatal consultations and cutting down on physical work during the last trimester of pregnancy; breast-feeding exclusively in the first 6 months after birth; giving children enriched porridge and mashed fruits beginning at 6 months of age; and making an extra effort to feed children with diarrhea or with other illnesses. Fathers, too, were expected to provide extra money for food, especially for pregnant or breast-feeding wives; to take on more of the workload, especially heavy physical labor; to support wives in making sure that they attended their prenatal visits; and to purchase healthier foods for the mothers and children.

The Burkina Faso project relied on a variety of media, including interpersonal communication, health center talks, radio, agricultural extension communication with men, literacy programs, and primary school programs. The interpersonal communication was primarily generated by the health workers themselves, either directly to each mother or through the health-center nutrition group-education sessions. Radio communications involved the use of a 20-episode radio drama centered around the same story line, tracking the daily lives of two Burkinan families. Subsequent health talk materials tracked the radio program episodes about these two families.

A program evaluation showed that more than half of the target population had been exposed to at least one of these sources of information. Health center-based interventions through the health worker outreach or health education talks reached fully 55% of the target women and 26% of the men. The radio was effective in reaching 41% of the target women and 60% of the men. In all, the communication resulted in a substantial increase in nutrition-related knowledge as well as behavioral improvements. A dose-response association was also found, with women responding especially to the health workers' talks and men to the radio spots. The radio programs were effective in increasing health-center attendance (especially prenatal visits), encouraging men to give more income to women to buy the promoted foods, and promoting the sharing of the nutrition messages with neighbors and relatives.

Mali. Baseline data from a second project in Mali (Parlato & Seidel, 1998) revealed that mothers delayed feeding of most solid foods until children were almost a year old. Neither mothers nor fathers were aware of women's or children's special dietary needs, and they tended to give priority to the adults who had "earned" better foods. Night blindness, a clinical sign of severe vitamin A deficiency, was highly prevalent.

As in the Burkina Faso experience, women were targeted with messages about appropriate nutrition during pregnancy and lactation, about breast-feeding and weaning foods, and about proper food choices to prevent and cure vitamin A deficiency. Both women and men were taught how to make healthy food choices in the marketplace. Interpersonal and group counseling were designed to reach the women, with a family health card including project messages and illustrated stickers (adapted from the Burkina Faso project described above). A radio show entitled *Elephant of the Desert* turned out to be an effective vehicle for promoting healthy nutrition. The show was so popular that the country's national radio station started broadcasting the series daily and even created new episodes.

The Mali project resulted in a reduction of acute malnutrition from 38% to 28% prevalence in intervention villages, whereas it remained unchanged in comparison villages. Chronic malnutrition and stunting were reduced from 46% to 31%. The proportion of children receiving colostrum doubled in program villages, while increasing about 35% in comparison villages. Mothers in intervention villages were also more likely to introduce porridge, fruit, green leafy vegetables, cow's milk, and meat or liver into their children's diets at an appropriate time following their sixth month. Dose-response relationships were also found, as exposure to the communication dose was correlated with the purchasing and consumption of healthier foods as well as better feeding practices. Cost-benefit analysis showed that the cost per child saved from underweight was $101, and $76 per child saved from stunting. Nearly 4,000 children's lives were saved as a result of the project, at less then $300 per life (Parlato & Seidel, 1998).

Niger. A third project in Niger promoted the consumption and production of vitamin A-rich foods among adults and young children. Formative studies identified locally available vitamin A food sources leading to the production of a calendar of seasonal sources for vitamin A as well as recommended portion sizes per type of person (man, mother, child) receiving the food. Four target audiences were approached: (a) men who purchased most of their families' food, (b) women who prepared and served the food, (c) commercial farmers who produced vitamin A-rich and other foods, and (d) health and extension agents. Specific behavioral targets were to increase the frequency with which liver was purchased as a snack for children and as a regular food stuff for children and wives, to encourage mothers to prepare and share 50 grams of liver with their child at least weekly, to increase the number of times children eat greens, and to increase the production of traditional greens in commercial gardens. Program planners had to keep seasonal timing in mind to ensure the availability and consumption of vitamin A-rich foods throughout the year. Specifically, children were targeted to eat greens every day and liver once a week.

Mass media had a limited reach in Niger. Therefore, interpersonal communication by the government health workers and agriculture extension agents was critical in promoting the message, as were skits presented by drama teams in each target village.

Results show that consumption of liver and vitamin A-rich greens grew significantly among women, but only slightly among children. Weekly liver consumption rose from 43% to 73% among women and from 37% to 49% among children. Interestingly, the villages with standard radio and interpersonal communication plus drama teams did not do as well as those who received only the radio and interpersonal communication (Parlato & Seidel, 1998).

SUMMARY

Nearly 200 million people worldwide are malnourished, most of them children. Yet, even in the world's poorest nations, growth monitoring and the promotion of breast-feeding can do much to alleviate suffering and reduce mortality due to malnutrition. Nutritional health communication by health workers supported by other media is central to increasing breast-feeding and improving growth monitoring. Where necessary, media advocacy and policy change must be used to limit formula advertisements. In summarizing the three West African experiences, Parlato and Gottert (1998) listed numerous recommendations for nutritional health-communication activities in minimally developed regions. These include the following:

1. Benefits to the behavior change must be discernible. Target behaviors that produce immediate responses (such as breast-feeding and oral rehydration) are more likely to be accepted than those that promise only long-term health changes.[1] In general, mothers want to see interventions that produce less illness among their children, and they want to see change relatively quickly. Growth-monitoring programs offer ideal sources of feedback and reinforcement for parents of infants and small children.

2. Two or three specific nutrition behaviors at the most should be targeted. Complex intervention messages that cover a smorgasbord of nutritional interventions and targets will be poorly understood and eventually rejected. Breast-feeding is an example of a straightforward behavioral target. Gradually, parents may learn about other foods rich in protein, energy, vitamins, and minerals that are readily available locally.

3. Messages should be disseminated as quickly as possible, with interpersonal and other media phased in to reinforce and support these messages. Health workers, extension agents, and other collaborators need not be engaged all at once, but all should be included eventually, as interpersonal communication may result in the longest term behavior change and less rejection of the overall message. Growth monitoring, specifically, implies the need for forceful and effective interpersonal communication, as does the promotion of breast-feeding, especially in the immediate postpartum phase.

4. Print and broadcast media can also be effective in taking the lead in or supplementing the overall communication effort. Print materials should be culturally appropriate, well-designed, and distributed through a reliable and broad network. Radio spots generally should be purchased, as free-of-charge time often results in spots being aired at unpopular times. Formula advertisements should generally be severely restricted or banned (Brown & Solomon, 1991; Jelliffe & Jelliffe, 1990).

FURTHER READING

Brown, K., & Solomon, N. (1991). Nutritional problems of developing countries. *Infectious Disease Clinics of North America, Edition on International Health,* 5(2), 297-317.

Jelliffe, D. B., & Jelliffe, E. F. P. (1990). *Growth monitoring in promotion in young children: Guidelines for the selection for the methods of training techniques.* New York: Oxford University Press.

Note

1. Notice the parallel to promoting "heart health" among young adults. Health promotion messages emphasizing life years gained through lower fat diets or aerobic activity have generally been replaced by those that focus on feeling and looking better.

4

Family Planning

Each modern decade witnesses faster increases in human population than at any previous point in history. The world's population, stable at under 1 billion for millennia, recently surpassed 6 billion and is expected at least to double again in the next century. In 1998, the world witnessed a net population gain of 84 million, or about 10,000 more inhabitants per hour (Reid, 1998). Population increases occur mostly in underdeveloped countries, which affects health in two ways: indirectly through degradation of the environment and natural resources of a region and directly through the decreased availability of human resources such as health care services. Even industrialized countries with low birth rates will absorb some of this population gain; the population of the United States is expected to increase from today's 260 million to over 400 million by 2050. Already heavily populated California will double its size in that same period of time.

Most of us believe that babies should have enough to eat; that we should live in a safe, clean environment; and that natural resources should be conserved, even if we do not always act consistently with these beliefs. Although there may be sharp disagreement about how to achieve it, most would also defend the notion of equality, or at least equal access to the potential for success. No societal issue, however, is as controversial as family planning. At community, regional, professional, and international levels, we remain sharply divided as to whether we should have population policies at all and, if so, how aggressively we should pursue them. Grounded in religious beliefs; sexual mores; suspicions about racism, gender, and socioeconomic inequalities; and the very definition of life itself, this debate has frozen policy makers and program developers domestically and abroad. The technology of behavior change applied to population control is especially loathsome to some religious and conservative political groups, who fear that public morality and freedom of choice will be severely compromised through formal population policies. Opposition to a family planning focus has made strange bedfellows among diverse groups, including the Catholic Church and Muslim clerics, free market and centralized market proponents, and even some women's rights advocates, who want this issue to be subordinated to women's health and gender equality (Potts, 1997).

For a variety of reasons, behavior-change approaches have come under attack by opponents of family planning (or at least those who oppose more aggressive approaches to population control). Yet, such approaches have been selected as interventions of choice by many program planners, given the fairly straightforward nature of birth control-related behaviors.

▨ Family Planning Interventions

Entertainment-education in Tanzania. A recent large-scale field trial in Tanzania employed an "entertainment-education" radio soap opera entitled *Twende na Wakati* (Let's Go With the Times) to promote the adoption of family planning (Rogers et al., 1999). Birth rates in the area where the soap opera was broadcast were compared to those in a control area elsewhere in the country. Tanzania's population more than tripled from 1948 to 1992, and the birth rate is six children per woman of reproductive age. Thus, the Tanzanian government adopted a target growth rate of 2% or less by the year 2010. *Twende na Wakati* is an important component of the overall strategy to reach that target.

The entertainment-education strategy is cast within social learning theory's emphasis on vicarious learning through the observation and imitation of role models and the reinforcement or punishment these models encounter as a function of their behavior. Three character types were employed in the soap opera: positive role models, negative role models, and transitional characters whose behavior gradually undergoes change over the course of the airing of the program. A man and wife who communicate openly about contraception and make firm plans to have a small family are rewarded with health and prosperity. The primary negative character is a promiscuous, alcoholic truck driver, who tries to hold on to numerous mistresses, eventually losing his wife, job, and life when he contracts HIV/AIDS. His wife, a transitional character, gradually takes control of her own reproductive and sexual health and makes a better life for herself and children. In 30-second epilogues following each show, the important behavioral messages are summarized (Rogers et al., 1999, p. 195). The show was broadcast twice weekly over a 2-year period, with a total of 204 episodes. Due to its popularity, broadcasts were resumed 2 years after they were initially suspended.

Scientific surveys demonstrated the effectiveness of *Twende na Wakati* for promoting family planning adoption. About 47% of the potential audience was exposed to the broadcast, listening to an average of over half of the episodes. A substantial majority of these individuals were favorably disposed to the program and were able to recall its key messages. One third of non-listeners talked about family planning frequently with their spouses, with 19% using contraceptives. Among listeners, these percentages were 85 and 64, respectively. Self-report data were validated by clinic information showing requests for contraceptives and reasons given. The authors conclude that the intervention was extremely successful in terms of both outcomes (safer sex, contraceptive use, and family planning) and the process used to reach the program goals (especially, increased communication between spouses).

Culturally tailored mass media in Mali. Across the continent from Tanzania, Mali is one of the poorest and least developed countries in the world. A decade ago, the prevalence of any form of contraception use in Mali was at most 7%, resulting in an annual population growth rate of 3%. Kane, Gueye, Speizer, Pacque-Margolis, and Baron (1998) report the results of a mass media campaign to promote contraceptive-related knowledge, attitudes, and behaviors among targeted married men and women in Bamako, the nation's capital and largest city (with a population of 900,000). The campaign, which addressed misconceptions, knowledge deficits, men's disapproval of family planning, and the perception that Islam is opposed to it, was conducted during the spring months of 1993.

The media mix included four television plays, four television commercials, and two recorded songs containing various family-planning messages, which were played on the radio during the intervention period. The plays aired twice, the short spots more than 40 times, and the two songs 70 or more times. These productions were supplemented by local live-theater shows with similar content. The content of the four plays included the following:

> *Play 1 (The Counseling):* Two couples go to family health clinics, one to adopt contraception and the other for infertility
>
> *Play 2 (Konami):* Two young girls become pregnant, and one dies. The theme is sexual responsibility. A masked image of a pregnant woman represents the village conscience of the community and reminds people about dangers of unwanted pregnancies and parent and community responsibility.
>
> *Play 3 (Let's Save Lives):* Two brothers are represented: one is well established and plans his family, the other has problems and does not. The intent is to stimulate discussion of the issue among men.
>
> *Play 4 (The Correct Measure):* This play puts contraception in the context of Islam and traditional healing. A couple goes to a traditional Muslim healer, whose advice turns out to be consistent with that later provided by a professional family-planning team.

The four 1-minute TV spots addressed similar themes: Couples need to communicate about family planning, they should not listen to rumor but instead talk to a professional, economic advantages are to be gained from having a limited number of children, and Islam does not oppose contraception (in this last spot, an Imam explains during prayers that couples should stop having children when they cannot support them) (Kane et al., 1998, p. 312). The theme of the songs were that birth spacing is good for children's health; breast-feeding women should delay further pregnancy to prevent malnutrition, weakness, and diseases; and families realize contentment through visits to the clinic and the adoption of contraception.

Kane et al. (1998) reported that as a result of the Mali project, self-reported modern contraceptive use among men increased from 26.9% to 29.6%, and female use from 11.8% to 15.4%. Surveys showed a substantial change in attitudes regarding the perception that Islam proscribes contraception. The authors concluded that campaigns using traditional theater, music, and proverbs in local languages and in familiar settings appear to be an effective way of creating a bridge between traditional cultural values and practices and the acceptance of new ideas.

A "conservative" Islamic revolution in Iran? Hoodfar and Assadpour (2000) provide an excellent account of long-term structural changes and communication strategies for the promotion of family planning. Probably to the surprise of many Westerners, these successes have been achieved in the Islamic Republic of Iran.

Although contraception has historically been accepted in Islam, the promotion of family planning by the U.S.-supported (and highly unpopular) Shah led to its denunciation by Muslim clerics. After the Shah was overthrown at the end of the 1970s, family planning was viewed as a Western imperialist plot to limit the growth of Muslim and other non-Christian countries. After the revolution, the black market in contraceptives continued in major cities. Nevertheless, the Ayatollah Khomeini's regime was initially pronatalist, and it dismantled the national family planning program.

Although the roles of men and women were strictly delineated in many ways, the Islamic government strongly advanced the cause of female education and improved national literacy rates in general. Infant mortality rates were cut by two thirds from 1974 to 1993 (Hoodfar & Assadpour, 2000, p. 21). These factors indirectly created the potential for increased contraception demand. Nevertheless, the legal age of marriage was lowered to the onset of puberty, and polygamy was allowed; together with the new pronatalist policies, this resulted in a rapid increase in fertility.

Although religious leaders had limited experience in governing and policy development (being barred from such roles by the Shah's government), technocrats in the government soon realized the potential negative impact of unlimited population growth on education, the economy, food and water supplies, and municipal services. They sought to influence the political religious leaders through a multipronged strategy, which emphasized the mobilization of public support through articles and interviews planted in local newspapers. Journalists soon discovered that the public was, indeed, highly interested in the topic, and coverage of the family planning issue was expanded. These same health and welfare experts gradually briefed religious leaders on the economic and public health implications of the rapid population growth, while acknowledging that moral aspects of population planning needed to be determined by the clerics. Eventually, a national conference was held among religious, health, and economic leaders, which resulted in a renewed national policy in 1989 (Hoodfar & Assadpour, 2000, p. 24).

Unlike the Shah's program, which emphasized the urban middle and working classes, Islamic support for the new program resulted in its promotion by rural clerics from the pulpit. Skilled speakers, as well as important conduits of communication among the rural poor, these clerics described the suffering caused by wasteful fertility and how such suffering is contrary to the principles of Islam. In urban areas, more than 40,000 volunteer women enthusiastically accepted responsibility for educating as many as 50 relatives, friends, and neighbors, thus greatly multiplying the overall communication effect. As a result, the overall fertility rate has decreased from 5.6 to 3.3 from 1985 to 1995, and the population growth rate went from 3.1% in 1966 to 3.4% in 1986 to 1.5 in 1996 (Hoodfar & Assadpour, 2000, p. 232).

Policy-Based Behavior Modification

Family-planning communications emphasizing only knowledge-attitude change approaches may be seen as inadequate by themselves without policy-based reinforcement to back them up, given the deep-rooted nature of practices related to family size. Conversely, the use of learning-theory-based procedures has often been associated with regimes (e.g., China) with highly centralized, ideologically based planning, which demands behavioral uniformity in entire populations. Clearly, the technology of behavior change on occasion has been used unscrupulously in various programs by practitioners and others. Yet, a full perspective needs to consider the entire context in which decisions to use this technology are made.

1. Behavior-change technology is not more manipulative than techniques based in other theories or social sciences. Many programs appeal to self control, attempt to achieve knowledge and attitude change among "pre-contemplators and contemplators" as precursors to behavior change, or emphasize norms or intentions rather than behavior per se. Yet, such programs are also based in deterministic models of behavior; if anything, they are only more subtle about how they approach it. No theory or model will be around long if it is not successful—social inoculation approaches to smoking prevention replaced health education efforts two decades ago, simply because knowledge-attitude-behavior (KAB) models (e.g., pictures of cancerous lungs and memorization of diseases related to smoking) were proven ineffective.

2. Reinforcement and other applications of learning theory are not unique to nor even "discovered" by behavioral psychology. Speed limits and high-occupancy vehicle lanes, salaries and time clocks, medals and courts-martial, grades and diplomas, frequent flier miles and tax deductions for home mortgages—all are accepted methods of behavioral engineering. In turn, these are built on naturally occurring contingencies, such as "please" and "thank you," desserts only after vegetables are eaten, and religion's proscription of sinful behavior.

3. Procedures based in learning theory, like other direct or indirect attempts to change behavior, are usually ineffective without community involvement in the planning and implementation of the technology. Thus, safeguards for their use

are needed to address not only ethical concerns but also very pragmatic ones. In the case of family planning, population surveys have shown that men and women in Latin America, Africa, and elsewhere want to limit their family size but are thwarted in doing so by limited access to safe and affordable contraception (Potts, 1997).

4. One half-million women die every year from pregnancy-related causes, virtually all of these being in the world's poorest countries (Jacobsen, 1983). Many times that number suffer serious health problems from planned and unplanned pregnancies and may contract sexually transmitted diseases that could have been prevented by contraceptive methods (Miller & Rosenfield, 1996). Sterilization programs, where available, are four times more costly for women than for men and pose less risk of complications for men. Yet, vasectomies are performed far less frequently than more invasive actions on women worldwide (Berelson, 1969). Abortions, often illegal and unsafe,[1] become the only option available for families seeking to limit their size but faced with an unplanned pregnancy.

Such naturally occurring aversive consequences will be accelerated over the coming century. The Earth's population, three times the level of 1900, may triple again by the year 2100. Starvation, uncontrollable epidemics, warfare, and environmental catastrophes may attenuate this growth, as may social and economic progress. If they do not, other options will become more and more limited as time goes on, with ever increasing likelihood that coercive restrictions on growth (such as the planet's longest-running family-planning program, China's One Child Policy) and migration will be applied. As Potts (1997) noted,

> The tragedy of China is that for ideological reasons the country delayed offering family planning choices for too long. The young women of today who are bullied by the commune into having abortions they do not want are the daughters of women who were denied the IUDs or sterilization they did want. (p. 10)

Fears about aversive forms of behavioral control may validate themselves over time if other actions are not taken. China's One Child Policy initially coined the phrase "one is best, at most two, never a third." Having two children was, at first, not penalized but only discouraged. In 1981, the policy was changed so that second births were forbidden, except under extraordinary circumstances. Enforcement was tightened, and positive reinforcement was replaced by coercive measures. Mandatory IUD insertions, abortions, and sterilizations were reported. Given progress as well as political change, the policy was relaxed in 1984. A greater emphasis was placed on community autonomy and on locally tailored goals. In the late 1980s, the policy was loosened further, taking preferences for male children into account. If the first child were a girl or disabled, or the parents were themselves only children, the family-planning cadres gave the couple permission for a second child. Many rural communities converted to a "two child" policy altogether. The population growth rebounded too strongly, and more restrictive policy was implemented again in the early 1990s (Short & Fengying, 1998). China's birth rate is now at about 1.9% (slightly below replacement levels) and stable.

Currently, the most common incentives for maintaining China's one-child level are cash subsidies (median U.S. $7 to $11 year for staying at or below the target birth rate, in the context of median annual household incomes at about $900). Other popular forms of subsidies (in order of frequency) are for child health, housing, and food. Fining couples for "out of plan" births is still frequent. Fines in 1993 were nearly $45 per birth (or 5% of the median household income). Apparently, a form of bureaucratic harassment, delayed registration of births, is also a common form of disincentive. In all, disincentives are more common than incentives, and have a far greater impact. Incentives appear to be less attractive to couples or villages, who would rather spend the money differently; however, fines levied are not always collected. Local policies are highly variable and currently in a high degree of flux (Short & Fengying, 1998).

The Promotion of Family Planning

Although learning-theory-based procedures, health communications, and social marketing approaches for promoting family planning and reducing wasteful fertility will continue to prove controversial, such programs can be both effective and ethical if developed within normal safeguards. Most family-planning programs promote increased contraceptive use and sterilization after a target family size has been reached. The latter, a form of "nonbirth" target, is preferred in large-scale programs, given the impossibility of monitoring condom, diaphragm, pill, and other contraceptive use (Rogers, 1973). Contraceptive sales data, for example, are highly suspect as markers of family-planning progress. Moreover, specific contraceptive targets (e.g., IUD-only programs) or sterilization limit freedom of choice in the target couple and increase the appearance of coercion and potential for rejection of a program.

Monetary incentives are the most frequent type of reinforcer included in family-planning programs. In a program in India in the mid-1950s, men were paid U.S. $7 to undergo vasectomies (Rogers, 1973). This resulted in 3.42 sterilizations per 1,000, more than three times the national average. Similar results were forthcoming in programs in Bangladesh and Sri Lanka, with participation directly related to the amount of compensation (Fincancioglu, 1982). Subsequent programs have used either nongraduated or graduated incentives. Graduated incentives may be applied in a variety of ways, such as lower payments for contraception versus sterilization or sterilization after many children versus after one or two. Such flexibility is likely to produce greater overall program success (Veatch, 1977).

Other forms of material reinforcers have included food supplements, clothing, or luxury items (Jacobsen, 1983). Social reinforcement through public recognition of both consumers and officials responsible for local efforts has resulted in maintenance of behavior change and the opportunity for vicarious learning.

Effective family planning programs, therefore, tend to specify a target family size and provide reinforcers based on whether a couple stays at or under that target. A prototype of this program comes from southern India, where payments of about a day's pay were made to women of childbearing age on their agreement to have no more than three children and to space these children by 3 or more years. Additional payments were made for each month of nonpregnancy and were redeemable when the woman reached the end of her childbearing years. Payments were graduated so that 2 years' worth were forfeited on the birth of a third child, 5 years after a fourth child, and the entire account after a fifth child was born. After the woman reached menopause, favorable prices were offered on retirement home plots if the agreement had been fulfilled. Birth rates on large tea estates where these families worked and resided fell dramatically over the years of these no-birth incentives, compared to rates in the country at large and at other tea estates without the incentives (Wallace, 1990).

Thailand's national and regional programs demonstrated substantial innovation in the use of incentives for child spacing. Incentives included assistance with animal raising, agriculture, and home industry. These incentives were made available through various arrangements, such as the provision of credit to purchase farm supplies at no interest. This cost was, in turn, deducted from future profits. Farm families who continued to participate in family planning were eligible to receive these credits. In one province, those who agreed to family planning were given a piglet upon engaging in a contingency contract in which they pledged to use birth control during the pig's 8-month fattening period. If they did not get pregnant in this time period, participating women were given an additional pig. At the end of 3 years, none of the participating women had given birth to another child.

Other nonbirth incentive programs have included an annual reward to married couples, preferential health care, schooling and housing, and retirement bonuses. Such approaches characterized the family planning efforts in Singapore three decades ago, which were so successful over the course of a generation that the program contributed to the total transformation of that society (Singh, Viegas, & Ratnam, 1985; Tan, Lee, & Ratnam, 1978). Today, so many women are placing an emphasis on their careers, later marriages, and few if any children that the government is promoting larger families to address the declining birth rate.

The Singapore experience also demonstrates the benefits of comprehensive packages for promoting family-planning adoption, which may include negative as well as positive reinforcement. In this national program, education, maternity leave, and social security benefits were withdrawn on the birth of a third child. Further analyses of Singapore adopters showed that women initially planning large families were especially influenced by housing benefits (or loss thereof), whereas working women were most interested in maternity leave (Singh et al., 1985; Tan et al., 1978). Tanzania's national program based contingencies on a fixed-interval schedule, with maternity leave granted only once every 3 years (Wallace, 1990).

Using change agents. As it has been for infectious disease and nutritional programs, the use of formal and informal change agents for family-planning promotion often has been shown to be effective. Specific methods of contraception used are strongly influenced by social network partners who are likely to use the same method. These influences are even more important than the woman's own individual characteristics (Valente, Watkins, Jato, van der Straten, & Tsitsol, 1997), indicating the need to focus on social network and interpersonal communication. Clinic personnel and program planners can take advantage of satisfied users to talk to women who remain ambivalent about the use of contraception, and they encourage each adopter to reach out to nonadopters in the network.

As Rogers (1973) points out, incentives for these "diffusers" may increase the rate of adoption of contraception by encouraging interpersonal communication with peers. A program in Sri Lanka used government field workers and previous adopters of IUDs as family-planning motivators. These teams were successful in recruiting later-adopters to accept the IUD as a family-planning method. In South Korea, a change-agent system encouraged informal communication about family planning within various communities. Different diffusers were recruited, including housewives, drugstore owners, beauticians, midwives, religious leaders, and village heads. Each change agent received about $15 for every IUD user recruited. This resulted in a 28% increase in IUD acceptance in targeted communities (Kwon, 1971).

Jacobsen (1983) noted that relatively small, one-time payments to family-planning acceptors and small payments to family-planning workers or doctors are the simplest and least expensive kind of payments to promote family planning. In Ghana, powdered milk was offered to both the family-planning field workers and the acceptors they recruited. Adding diffuser incentives resulted in a tripling of patients attending family-planning clinics.

Equality Issues

Inequality is every bit as much at work in wasteful fertility as it is in infectious diseases and malnutrition. Perhaps in no other public health issue does social (especially gender) inequality play such an important role. Worldwide, a woman's recognition comes primarily from motherhood and not from being a coequal in the community at large. Over half of all women and girls in the world live under conditions that threaten their health, deny them choice about childbearing, limit educational attainment, restrict economic participation and productivity, and even offer them fewer civil rights than their brothers and husbands (Fathalla, 1990). Violence against women can directly harm reproductive health (Miller & Rosenfield, 1996). Interventions that directly or indirectly promote the status of women not only may be as effective as incentive approaches to reducing wasteful fertility but also may portend a far broader positive impact on society as a whole.

Education. In developing countries, women generally have lower literacy rates than men, a strong predictor of infant mortality and other health indices (Miller & Rosenfield, 1996). Education is one of the most reliable predictors of fertility and probably the single strongest influence on a woman's control of her future. Expansion of female enrollment, counseling and follow-up for drop-outs, and the incorporation of family-planning and women's issues in school curricula may optimize both the participation in and the benefit from public schooling. Should formal schooling not prove feasible for political reasons, the use of distributed learning to reduce the 25% worldwide illiteracy rate among women would accomplish some of the same goals.

Women in the labor force. "Women's work," traditionally home and child care and agricultural labor, is undervalued in most societies (Miller & Rosenfield, 1996). The single most important component of the demographic transition in industrializing countries (see Chapter 8) is the entry of women into the traditionally male workforce, which in turn contributes to the decision to have smaller families. Although the economic advantages of this decision may be a factor for many women making it, the more critical mechanism appears to be the delay of marriage that attends it. Women employed in the modern industrial or professional sector marry at an average of 2.4 years later than those doing domestic or agricultural work.

Inequality issues can be addressed through a variety of methods. Access to financial resources, for example, small loans to women in rural areas for purposes of beginning businesses, has been shown to improve reproductive health (Miller & Rosenfield, 1996). Social marketing, media advocacy, and community self-control must all be applied to reducing the second-class status of half of the world's population. Once progress is realized in equality, family-planning progress also will be achieved.

SUMMARY

More than most health promotion programs, family-planning procedures rely on modifying behavior-consequence relationships, either vicariously through role models and the media or directly through policies encouraging small family size.

Substantial progress has been made in many nations in the promotion of family planning and the reduction of wasteful fertility. A lack of women's rights, combined with women's inequality, hampers progress in other countries. Nevertheless, substantial contributions can be made by improving services for family planning and promoting their use.

Simmons and colleagues (1997) have suggested the following framework that takes into account user, service, and technology variables for planning optimal clinic services, health communication, and learning-theory-based procedures for promoting contraception and family planning:

User variables: Reproductive health needs and rights, users' perspectives, medical profiles, and sociocultural and gender influences. Specific attention must be paid to the physical and emotional needs of the mother as well as her right to make reproductive choices in the first place.

Service variables: Policies, program structure, personnel facilities, management, availability and accessibility of services and quality of care. Family planning as well as primary health care services in general must be attractive and available to the consumer if program success is to be achieved.

Technology: Method mix, efficacy, side effects, administration, reversibility, and duration. The best contraceptive services are those that maximize the woman's choice and ease of adoption and minimize her present or future risks.

FURTHER READING

The reader is encouraged to review various journals that address family planning issues, programs, and research, especially *Studies in Family Planning.*

▓ Note

1. Unsafe abortions are defined by the World Health Organization as procedures conducted by people lacking the necessary skills or in an environment lacking minimal standards (Miller & Rosenfield, 1996, p. 377).

5

Infectious Diseases

Emerging and re-emerging infectious diseases have received ample media coverage the past few years. AIDS, Lyme disease, Ebola, hantavirus, and drug-resistant strains of tuberculosis have raised the specter of uncontrollable international epidemics. Yet biological and epidemiological studies of these diseases have, at times, overlooked the critical role of social and behavioral factors in the spread and control of infectious diseases. For example, destruction of natural habitats and their replacement with golf courses contributes greatly to the spread of Lyme disease, whereas agricultural and other economic development has provided fertile opportunities for other microbes. Conversely, malaria, today considered a "tropical disease," was a major killer of Americans until the last century, with a reach as far north as the Ohio River Valley (Farmer, 1996). The decline of malaria in North America can be attributed more to agricultural expansion and the reduction of inequalities in the region's population than to specific malaria-control efforts.

This chapter presents programs that address some of the world's most deadly infectious diseases (with the exception of HIV/AIDS, which is discussed by itself in the following chapter). Infectious diseases comprise a broad category of illnesses that particularly threaten populations in developing countries, especially children under 5 years old. Infectious diseases can be transmitted in diverse ways, including through water, food, air, vectors, sexual activity, and bodily fluids. The prevention and control of infectious diseases will vary widely, depending on the type of transmission and behaviors involved in contracting and preventing the infection. The spectrum of prevention ranges from control to eradication, with the following definitions (Dowdle & Hopkins, 1998):

Control: The reduction of disease incidence, prevalence, morbidity, and mortality to acceptable levels as a result of planned interventions, the maintenance of which are required to sustain the reduction.

Disease elimination: Reduction of disease incidence to zero within defined geographic areas as a result of interventions, the maintenance of which is required.

Infection elimination: Reduction of infection due to a specific agent to zero in a defined geographic area, as a result of a specific intervention. Continued efforts are needed to prevent the re-establishment of transmission.

Eradication: Permanent reduction of *worldwide* disease incidence caused by reduction of a specific agent to zero as a result of specific interventions, which are no longer needed.

Extinction: The specific agent exists neither in the laboratory nor in nature.

This chapter focuses on behavior-change interventions for the prevention and control of the infectious diseases that, together with AIDS, are major threats to the health of adults, but more important are the primary killers of children under 5 throughout the world: vaccine-preventable diseases, diarrhea, acute respiratory infections, tuberculosis, and vector-borne diseases.

Interventions

Vaccine-Preventable Diseases

Twenty years ago, the World Health Assembly officially declared that smallpox had been eradicated, the only time in human history that such a victory could be declared (Hinman, 1999). Poliomyelitis is currently being targeted for eradication, with measles, perhaps, being next in line. Factors affecting the potential for disease eradication include:

- Highly effective, safe, stable, and preferably inexpensive vaccines
- Lifelong immunity after immunization or natural infection
- Short period of communicability
- Easily identifiable set of clinical symptoms for ease of surveillance
- Easy and reliable diagnostic procedures
- Absence of an environmental reservoir of the infectious agent
- Causal agent that is genetically stable
- Seasonal occurrence (Hinman, 1999; Stuart-Harris, Western, & Chamberlayne, 1982)

Thus, some vaccines are not likely to result in eradication, including those for hepatitis B (infection that results in a lifelong carrier state), meningitis (limited vaccine effectiveness and high cost), *haemophilus influenzae* Type b (Hib) (high cost), plague and Japanese B encephalitis (permanent animal reservoir), diphtheria (not feasible with current toxoid), tuberculosis (transmission is not affected), typhoid (long carrier state), influenza (the virus mutates frequently), streptococcus pneumoniae (limited effectiveness), and pertussis (unknown effectiveness for controlling transmission by adults). The eradication of hepatitis A, mumps, and rubella are biologically feasible, but the campaign awaits decisions by public health officials worldwide to invest the resources necessary to conquer these diseases (Hinman, 1999).

Vaccine-preventable diseases are among the most common and deadly killers of young children, and vaccines to achieve control of these diseases are inexpensive and relatively easy to use. Indeed, immunization programs are recognized as perhaps the most cost-effective of all public health interventions (Kim-Farley, 1992). However, as late as 25 years ago, fewer than 5% of children in developing countries were adequately immunized against diphtheria, tetanus, pertussis, measles, polio, and tuberculosis. These diseases are especially deadly when combined with malnutrition, as the child's resistance is generally lower, and the health care needed to combat diseases once they do occur is generally inadequate. Over the past century, in contrast, the United States has witnessed between 97% (tetanus) and 100% (polio) reductions in these diseases (Hinman, 1999). Over 3 million deaths per year are being prevented through vaccination against measles, pertussis, and neonatal tetanus alone (Cutts, 1998).

Vaccine-preventable diseases strike primarily in infancy; therefore, the window of opportunity for vaccination is open for only a short period of time. Community coverage is made difficult by the fact that most vaccines require refrigeration, and services are not typically mobile without appropriate (and expensive) equipment. Generally, vaccines for diphtheria, pertussis, and tetanus (DPT) as well as polio must be given at three different times, although the number and frequency of boosters depends on the disease patterns, health services infrastructure, resources, and health priorities of a given country (Cutts, 1998, p. 446). Educating and motivating parents to return for further immunizations is often difficult, which leaves their children unprotected.

Delivery sites for vaccinations will also vary. Fixed sites such as clinics and health posts are preferred for logistical reasons, but mobile units may be necessary to achieve coverage in remote areas. In either case, attendance will be optimized if services are presented courteously with little waiting time and in conjunction with other curative care (Cutts, 1998).

Mass campaigns versus regular services. Many countries will elect to supplement regular immunization campaigns with national immunization days, backed heavily by media campaigns and sponsorship by political officials. Others see such campaigns as being imposed by foreign donors, who are looking for the maximum public relations value without regard to whether regular health services are being disrupted. Experiences in West African countries have been mixed at best, although Latin America has realized success with national *jornadas* (special campaigns of limited duration), especially when implemented with local funding. At present, national campaigns are used primarily to supplement long-term disease-control efforts rather than to reach some immediate goal (Cutts, 1998, p. 447).

Learning-theory-based procedures for smallpox elimination in India. One of the greatest public health victories in history involves the worldwide eradication of smallpox (Hinman, 1999). The control of smallpox in India was accomplished, in part, through general community surveillance underpinned, in some cases, by incentive systems (Basu & Jezek, 1978; Pan American Health Organization/WHO, 1986; Pillsbury, 1990). Smallpox surveillance was facilitated by highly visible symptoms and scars left on previous victims. Communities where individuals evidenced scars but where there were no new active cases (especially among the very young) could be certified as disease-free (Davey, 1997, p. 27). Surveillance teams and allied health workers were trained to visit villages and (a) report fever cases with rashes, (b) conduct special searches in high-risk and/or remote areas, (c) conduct searches at public markets where relatively large numbers of people can be found in a small period of time, and (d) multiply their effectiveness by soliciting government employees, teachers, postmen, and others to assist in the surveillance. To help promote the surveillance, each worker earned a financial bonus for successful detection. Citizens at large apparently were eligible for a variety of reinforcers as well, which greatly improved all forms of surveillance.

Although the reward publicity included the use of wall markings, posters, media advertisements, and loudspeakers, the most effective form of publicizing the reinforcer itself was word-of-mouth information from health workers or others. Loudspeakers were the second-most effective approach, especially in open areas, markets, and other crowded locations. To improve the discrimination of the surveillance, citizens and workers were provided with "recognition cards" depicting people stricken specifically with smallpox and not chickenpox or related illnesses. Apparently, both rewards and marketplace targets were effective. Thus, a quarter of a century ago, field research was demonstrating the effectiveness of behavior modification backed by village-level media in tackling one of the greatest scourges of all time.

Comprehensive promotion of immunization in Ecuador. Compared to many health behaviors, immunization represents a straightforward target. It is highly effective, observable, and noncontroversial in medical and political circles. Nevertheless, three factors contribute to an underuse of immunizations: (a) avoidance created by fear of injections and the negative side effects (e.g., fever, swelling) of vaccinations; (b) competing priorities mothers have, which may preclude taking their children in to be immunized; and (c) the lack of immediate reinforcement inherent in this (or any) prophylactic procedure. Health-promotion interventions need not only to address the lack of knowledge related to immunizations, but also to reduce barriers to bringing children to health centers for immunization.

In 1986, a vaccination campaign in Ecuador sought to address these three factors to increase DPT vaccine coverage throughout the country. Comic books, radio spots (with time donated by the stations), and modeling by highly recognizable personalities promoted an increase in knowledge and reduction of fears concerning vaccinations. Actual immunization efforts were channeled into periodic campaigns (*jornadas*) in which the primary health care system focused its energies and resources on making immunizations as convenient as possible for a few specific days. High school students posted over 250,000 awareness/announcement posters and delivered to mother's homes calendars that had been marked with dates of the vaccinations. The Ministry of Health, National Institute for the Child and Family, armed forces, Ministry of Education, oil companies, foreign donors, and others all contributed to the mobilization of the campaign. Diplomas were given to mothers whose children were completely vaccinated, with additional gold stars affixed to them when vaccinations were completed before the age of 1. In all, these efforts resulted in vaccinations for over a half million children (Elder et al., 1994, pp. 343-344).

Polio: On the verge of eradication. Like other viruses, polio can multiply only by invading a cell and using the cell's own mechanism for replication. Hence, once immunization deprives the virus of its human host, polio will rapidly die out (Davey, 1997). The four-fold strategy to eradicate polio includes high routine immunization coverage, supplementary immunizations with national immunization days or campaigns, effective surveillance, and, finally, "mopping up" operations through door-to-door immunization efforts in areas where the infection persists. Where the disease is thought to be controlled, continued surveillance is needed until worldwide eradication is achieved.

This combination of approaches led to polio being eradicated in the Americas by 1994. Remarkably, this was accomplished in spite of endemic civil wars in several American regions, including El Salvador, Peru, Colombia, and Nicaragua. In these countries, one-day "immunization truces" were called and observed by all combatants. These truces in the Americas and elsewhere were due in part to the advocacy of Rotary International, which has used community organization and social marketing to help promote polio immunizations. Worldwide, the number of polio cases decreased from 35,251 in 1988 to 3,755 in 1996.

Diarrheal Diseases

Diarrhea is a symptom of a number of intestinal diseases, including viral, bacterial, or parasitic infections. There is no thought of ever eliminating these diseases: Virtually all children get diarrhea at some or many points in their infancy and childhood. However, diarrheal disease is a leading cause of infant and child death in the world, with 5 million children dying from it every year.

Dehydration is generally the direct cause of death due to diarrhea. The risk of mortality increases during weaning, as the child is less protected from contamination that may be present in weaning foods but not in breast milk. Malnutrition and diarrhea are components of a vicious cycle that may result in mortality, as a child's overall resistance is worn down, and the child may succumb easily to the disease.

Diarrhea and especially dehydration, however, are easily controllable. Oral rehydration through the use of water-sugar-salt solutions or premixed oral rehydration salts (ORS) is a well-proven method for preventing or controlling dehydration. Bottle feeding, uncovered food and unpurified water, and uncovered toilets and trash are among the risk factors for diarrhea. Personal hygiene, clean water supply, clean foodstuffs, and breast-feeding will lower the risk of diarrhea or the risk of suffering from it. Again, none of these factors can be fully addressed without active human behavioral involvement.

Bangladesh's BRAC program. The BRAC program (see also p. 83) in Bangladesh, one of the world's poorest and most overpopulated nations, is one of the longest-standing and most successful programs in the history of public health promotion. Following the development of oral rehydration solutions for preventing dehydration, BRAC eventually imparted the knowledge and skills necessary to mix water, salt, and unrefined brown sugar and properly administer the fluids to 12 million households throughout the country. Health professionals initially thought that it would be impossible to teach illiterate mothers how to mix ORS

This Honduran health worker demonstrates the steps of mixing oral rehydration salts to a homemaker.

with ingredients available in the home. Young female multipliers, most of them also mothers, were mobilized to teach the skill through door-to-door interpersonal communication. These multipliers were eligible to receive monetary reinforcers when monitors tested to see that the mothers they trained had memorized the messages and could demonstrate the mixing skills (Mustaque, Chowdhury, & Cash, 1996).

Interpersonal communication and contingency management in Gambia. The HealthCom Project, carried out by the Academy for Educational Development (1995), examined a variety of social marketing and other health-promotion efforts in developing countries around the world. One target country was Gambia, a West African nation whose population is largely illiterate and has limited access to mass media or transportation. In Gambia, a flyer was developed depicting how to mix a sugar-water-salt solution to treat dehydration and save the lives of young children suffering from diarrhea. Village women who had been trained by health workers to promote the oral rehydration program received a bright-colored flag to display over their homes, indicating their expertise in this area. The sugar-salt-water mixing ingredients were promoted by them and via the radio. Mixing contests were held around the country over a 5-week period, reinforcing women with a small prize if they were able to show that they knew how to mix the ORS solution correctly. In addition, villages with a high percentage of mothers who were able to demonstrate that they could mix ORS received community-based prizes, such as radios. This effort resulted in a substantial increase in knowledge and a reduction in purging or other harmful practices related to diarrheal treatment (Elder et al., 1994, p. 342).

Skill development in Indonesia. Oral rehydration is a complicated procedure and not easily mastered by minimally trained health workers (in Indonesia known as *kader*), let alone by mothers. In West Java (Indonesia), village health workers are often volunteers selected by village chiefs for this work. Thus, their training is minimal and, unfortunately, often unaccompanied by a lack of confidence in their skills as health workers.

The HealthCom effort (Academy for Educational Development, 1995) in West Java addressed these issues by developing counseling cards for village health workers to help them diagnose the severity of diarrhea and dehydration and to promote the correct mixing and administration of oral rehydration or other interventions needed to treat the child. The counseling card set consisted of five colored cards. The first card was a binary decision tree by which the health worker could establish the correct level of severity of the child's symptoms. The severity was matched to a specific color, which corresponded with a color-coded card. This card, then, told the health worker what to say to the mother with respect to the child's diarrhea, use of oral rehydration solution, continued breast-feeding, or need to seek immediate medical attention if the symptoms were extreme. Health workers using the cards were substantially more effective than health workers trained through traditional didactic methods without benefit of the cards' sustained "portable supervision" (Elder et al., 1992).

Social marketing in Kenya. In an innovative effort by Kenya and colleagues (1990), a community-wide oral rehydration therapy intervention campaign centered in social marketing techniques was conducted in a district of western Kenya. The evaluation of this campaign compared the use of a "value-added product" (flavored rather than unflavored ORS) sold through private outlets and combined with distribution of free unflavored packets through primary care centers. In a control district, only unflavored ORS packets were distributed, again free-of-charge, through primary health care facilities.

During the campaign, private mobile cinema companies showed a film promoting the free unflavored packets at the clinics and the flavored packets for sale through pharmacies and other commercial outlets. To promote the selling of the packets in retail outlets, an incentive system for shopkeepers was devised with the following elements: (a) shopkeepers purchased the salts from wholesalers using cash rather than credit, motivating them to move their stock quickly; (b) shopkeepers were granted an acceptable profit margin; and (c) volume discounts were also available. More important, shopkeepers were allowed to explain to the mothers how to use the salts appropriately, and they were given promotional materials to advertise the salts (which sold at about four packets for U.S. 35 cents). The packets were priced consistently with over-the-counter medications for diarrhea, so as not to make them look too inexpensive.

To launch the campaign, local officials and chieftains held a public rally where they jointly prepared an ORS mixture and drank it in front of a large audience. Promoters then distributed premixed solutions for taste-testing in neighborhoods throughout the study area. During the campaign, the film was shown at public places during regular intervals.

The study showed that at the end of the campaign, over half of the households in the intervention district self-reported that they had on at least one occasion administered ORS; this result was statistically superior to use of ORS in households in the control district. Primary care centers distributed 13,500 free packets, less than two thirds of the 21,600 packets that were sold through the retailers. Therefore, it appears that sales through the shops created a substantially higher demand for oral rehydration solutions. The cinema intervention, however, the primary medium for the social marketing campaign, appeared to have had only minimal direct impact on sales. Only about 14% of the experimental households remembered having seen the movie. Overall, the households in the experimental district also administered more ORS per episode than did households in the control area.

The authors contrast their experience to another oral rehydration campaign in Egypt. In the Egyptian program, pharmacists and shopkeepers were not trained to educate mothers how to use ORS, even though they were given the opportunity to sell packets. Also, the packets were provided to the retail outlets free-of-charge, and the pharmacists were instructed to sell the packets at a nominal price rather than at a price that was competitive with other over-the-counter products. This may have been insufficient to motivate the shopkeepers or to appear worthwhile to consumers. In Egypt, the communication campaign to promote oral rehydration was conducted door-to-door rather than via a mass communication approach. However, it is not clear that either effort was particularly effective. Looking at both the Kenyan and Egyptian experiences, the authors conclude that private sector availability and promotion of ORS can serve as a valuable complement to public sector availability.

Acute Respiratory Infections (ARIs)

ARIs are the second-leading cause of child mortality in the world and one of the most prevalent illnesses. Among children under 5 years old, 4 million deaths annually may be attributed to ARIs, most of which are specifically due to pneumonia. Upper respiratory infections consist of colds, otitis media, and tonsillitis, whereas lower respiratory infections include laryngitis and bronchiolitis in addition to pneumonia. Risk factors for ARIs and especially for pneumonia include being under the age of 2 or over 65, suffering from poor nutritional status, having low birth weight, not being breast-fed, being exposed to smoking or other forms of air pollution, living in an environment that is crowded, and having incomplete immunization or vitamin A deficiency (Stansfield & Shepard, 1993).

Although severe ARI cannot be treated in the home, the quickness of parental response to early symptoms can be critical in saving the life of the child. A simple cold or cough with no stridor (a harsh, vibrating sound heard when air passages are obstructed) or fast breathing may disappear fairly quickly. However, if the cough is persistent for a month or more, or if a severe earache, sore throat, or fever are manifest, pneumonia may be indicated. Ensuring that the child is warm and continues to get plenty of fluids in regular feeding during the ARI can contribute to survival rates. Pneumonia may be handled at home with antibiotics if the fever is treated and there is no chest indrawing or fast breathing. Chest indrawing indicates the need to refer to a hospital immediately for antibiotic and fever treatment. An inability to drink, convulsions, abnormal sleeping patterns, or stridor may indicate a more severe pneumonia, which will have to be treated with more urgency.

Comprehensive behavioral interventions for ARI management in Honduras. A promising combination of communication and learning-theory-based techniques comes from a Honduran study that has shown the effectiveness of the use of radio in training populations or professionals in various adaptive behaviors. These target populations are often in areas that are difficult to access. Media-based education, therefore, may supplement educational techniques that health workers or others are using. Health workers can be made aware of a particular time for a radio broadcast and can organize a group of mothers or others to listen to the broadcast together. Subsequently, the health workers might lead a discussion of the information and perhaps even practice the skills prescribed during the broadcast with the group.

An ARI intervention conducted in Honduras emphasized health worker skills in promoting behavior change among mothers, who learned how to detect and manage ARIs in their children. The ultimate target behaviors included recognizing the symptoms of ARI, keeping the nasal passage clear and the baby fed, and taking the child to the health center immediately if symptoms worsened. The specific skills promoted among the health workers involved getting mothers to practice ARI management skills and receive positive recognition in clinic *charlas* (health talks). Mothers who attended these charlas were encouraged to share the health information with their neighbors. In turn, knowledge sharing was reinforced with village-wide lotteries, whereby mothers who could respond to three ARI-management questions received small prizes. Following the success of this intervention in four pilot regions, health workers throughout the nation were taught how to implement similar training and motivational procedures for ARI control in their catchment areas.

Tuberculosis

Between 6 million and 8 million individuals contract tuberculosis each year, with about 2 million deaths (Dye, Garnett, Sleeman, & Williams, 1998; Murray & Salomon, 1998a, 1998b). One third of the world's population is currently infected with tuberculosis (Porter & McAdam, 1994). Tuberculosis is the seventh-leading cause of premature mortality and disability in the world (Murray & Lopez, 1997a). Eastern European countries evidence particularly high incidence rates. Due to its strong interaction with HIV, tuberculosis is on the rise in Africa and Asia, as well. Given the appearance of drug-resistant strains, tuberculosis will likely remain one of the world's biggest killers for the foreseeable future.

Paradoxically, inexpensive and effective therapy has been available for tuberculosis for some time. Accusing developed nations of being apathetic toward the disease, Grange and Zumla (1999) cite three reasons for this apathy: first, tuberculosis is no longer seen as a problem in the West, even with the increased incidence in the United States and Europe; second, tuberculosis is highly related to poverty, which is expected to diminish in the developing world (when the opposite may be true); and third, the principal barrier to eliminating the disease is seen as patient noncompliance (when inadequate health care may actually be the culprit). In any case, vigorous action is required to contain and reduce the spread of this dread disease.

Prevention holds even greater potential for global tuberculosis control. By ensuring that active cases are diagnosed as early as possible (case finding) and isolated until successfully treated with an antibiotic regimen (case holding), public health efforts can protect uninfected individuals. Ideally, patients should be hospitalized during the isolation phase, but this is not practical in many of the world's poorer regions. In such cases, the medical intervention should include the semi-isolation of patients at home, where they avoid contact with others, especially susceptible individuals (e.g., children and individuals who are HIV-positive) and avoid the public in general except in spacious, outdoor settings. The contagious period usually lasts for up to 2 weeks following the beginning of therapy (Menzies, Tannenbaum, & FitzGerald, 1999).

The BCG vaccination reduces the risk of active tuberculosis, once infection occurs. Currently, nearly 88% of all infants worldwide receive this vaccination. However, compliance with the medical regimen is the single most important factor in assuring the recovery of the patient and preventing the spread of the disease. In resource-rich environments, this process entails frequent visits to the physician, urine tests, and pill counts (Menzies et al., 1999). Such an approach is less practical in most developing countries, where the WHO has advocated the "directly observed therapy—short term" (DOTS) approach (Dye et al., 1998; Gleissberg, 1999). In this procedure, passive case detection (the patient presents with an illness and is then diagnosed to have tuberculosis) is followed by a chemotherapy regimen in which the health worker actually observes the patient consuming the medication in the clinic or the patient's home.

Of additional relevance to the design of behavioral interventions is the containment of an outbreak of tuberculosis. This is enhanced through contact investigation, the third priority in tuberculosis control behind case finding and case holding (Menzies et al., 1999). In this process, an evaluation of the patient's living environment takes place, with special attention to crowding and ventilation. Susceptible individuals who live or sleep with the infected patient, as well as other close contacts (e.g., school or work mates), are encouraged to undergo testing at two different intervals, with appropriate therapeutic follow-up as needed.

Multipliers and incentives for community control of tuberculosis in Bangladesh. Treatment adherence and tuberculosis cure have been promoted successfully by lay volunteers and church groups in the Philippines, women's organization volunteers in Indonesia, and former patients in Haiti (Maher, Van Gorkom, Gondrie, & Raviglione, 1999). However, much remains to be learned about the use of indigenous workers and natural healers in tuberculosis-control programs. Although best known for its effective promotion of oral rehydration therapy, the BRAC program in Bangladesh (p. 77) has also been applied to tuberculosis screening and control. Again, physicians and other community health workers work with largely young and illiterate village women to tackle health problems in the poorest communities of this impoverished nation (Chowdhury, 1999). These village women receive 2 weeks to 1 month of training, with monthly in-service boosters. No salary is offered, although they do retain a small profit from their sales of prescribed drugs and incentives related to detecting and following up on specific diseases.

Each of the 4,500 workers covers about 200 households, distributing tuberculosis information through village meetings and posters. They look for individuals who have had a cough for 4 weeks or longer, and they collect early morning sputum samples, which are taken to the local laboratory for testing. Positive patients are contacted by professional health workers and encouraged to register for treatment (Chowdhury, Chowdhury, Islam, Islam, & Vaughan, 1997).

Incentives are as central to the BRAC approach to tuberculosis control as they are to its diarrheal program. Patients who are registered for treatment pay a deposit of (U.S. equivalent) $5, half of which is refunded on successful completion of the treatment regimen; the other half is given to the BRAC worker (Chowdhury, 1999). The worker also receives U.S. 60 cents for each new case she identifies. If the patient does not complete the therapy, the worker still retains her share of the deposit, with the remainder retained by the BRAC program.

Evaluation of the BRAC tuberculosis-control program shows it to be extremely effective. The acceptance of the treatment regimen among diagnosed patients was over 90%, and the cure rate for a sample of 1,741 patients was 85.3%, with only a 2.4% default rate. Population surveys showed a prevalence rate in two communities with the BRAC program at less than half of a community without it. The authors justifiably conclude that a volunteer system backed by incentives and a professional staff is essential to controlling tuberculosis in poor societies. In Bangladesh, perhaps as many as half of all patients who begin tuberculosis treatment do so because of the BRAC program. Plans are to extend the program to communities with 25 million inhabitants (Chowdhury et al., 1997).

Vector Control

Vector-borne diseases are those that are transmitted by one organism (the vector) from one infected individual (host) to another, without necessarily affecting the vector itself. Vectors may include mosquitoes, fleas, rats, mice, or other carriers with which humans have contact. Vector-control strategies include eradicating the vector and its source, minimizing contact between the vector and the host, providing the host a prophylactic in case contact does occur, and isolating an infected host so that further spread does not occur. Again, each of these strategies is either partially or fully dependent on human behavior change.

Typically, however, approaches to vector control involve vertical programs (i.e., those designed and implemented by health officials, requiring no active participation by the population) to reduce the source of transmission. For example, yellow fever and malaria eradication programs primarily rely on the eradication of the mosquitoes implicated in these diseases. Specifically, larval production sites and house spraying with systemic insecticides can be successful, if substantial administrative and political support is provided. However, for many vectors, such eradication constitutes only short-term control, as areas will become reinfested in a fairly short period of time. Thus, vertical control programs may be ineffective because communities are not active partners in the control but rather passive participants or recipients of the eradication effort (Gubler, 1989). Therefore, the challenge for vector control is not whether source reduction is effective but whether and how community participation can be a part of that source reduction effort (Lloyd, 1991).

Vector control differs substantially from control of chronic disease and other infectious disease in many ways. Vector control requires independent, individual behavior change just as chronic disease and infectious disease prevention do;

Uncontrolled garbage dumps such as this provide ideal breeding locations for mosquitoes.

however, vector control cannot be effective (or at least very effective) if carried out only on an individual basis. Thus, if rats, mosquito-breeding sites, or other vectors and their sources are eliminated in one household but not in the neighbors', the individuals in that cleaner household are likely to receive little added protection from the diseases these vectors carry. At some point, however, a critical mass may be reached where a sufficient number of vectors are eliminated in an area or region, thereby reducing everyone's risk for contracting the vector-borne disease.

Background: The malaria vector. An examination of malaria transmission is instructive for a general understanding of vector-borne diseases and how human behavior interacts with their transmission. Malaria results from an infection by parasites of the genus *Plasmodium.* Human transmission occurs through the bite of the *Anopheles* mosquito.[1] The infecting parasite is injected into the blood with the saliva of the biting mosquito. Within a half hour, the sporozoites invade liver tissue cells, where they multiply. They then invade red blood cells, after having multiplied to tens of thousands of times their initial number. This part of the cycle occurs in 1 to 2 weeks, depending on the type of parasite.

Disease symptoms are caused by the parasites in the blood. Later, transition from the liver to the blood may result in repeated relapses, as most antimalarial drugs clear the blood of parasites but are not effective against those in the liver.

Like other mosquitos, the Anopheles variety lives primarily around water. Eggs are laid on the edge of the water and hatch in 2 to 3 days to produce larvae. Larvae eventually develop into pupae and then into flying adult mosquitos. Depending on the species, water-breeding sites may vary from permanent to transient, fresh to brackish, standing to flowing, open sun to shade, and from shallow pools to deep wells.

The primary symptom of malaria is fever of variable severity, with days of lesser or no symptoms. Fever occurs in three stages: cold shivering, burning dry skin, and drenching sweat. Repeated infections generally give rise to an immune response. However, fever due to the *Plasmodium falciparum* parasite can rapidly result in death. Warning signs include shock, anemia, convulsions, spontaneous bleeding, pulmonary edema, or respiratory distress. The risk of severe illness from malaria is primarily among those who have no immunity and, therefore, especially among children under the age of 2.

About 270 million people annually are infected with malaria parasites, and 110 million of them will develop clinical symptoms. Equatorial regions of Latin America, Africa, and Asia suffer from the highest malaria incidence, with most deaths occurring in tropical Africa. Nevertheless, one of the crucial effects of malaria is on productivity rather than mortality per se, as the illness saps a person's energy and ability to work. Days of disability per case of malaria may range from 5 to 20.

According to Negerá, Liese, and Hammer (1993), there are three general malaria-control measures designed to prevent epidemics and reduce the endemic level of malaria. First is the reduction of human-mosquito contacts through the use of bed nets, repellents, protective clothing, and window and door screens in the houses. Second, domestic control spraying may reduce the number of adult mosquitos, whereas mosquito larvae can be controlled or eliminated through peridomestic sanitation, regular drying of water containers, larvicide for water surfaces, alternation of crop irrigation with fallow, dry periods, and biological control (e.g., through the use of fish or turtles to consume mosquitoes and their pupae). Finally, source reduction involves sanitation, small-scale drainage in the home and property environment, and community-wide drainage and water management. Unfortunately, the Anopheles has developed resistance to biochemical control measures, as have the parasites they transmit. Communities have become pessimistic about the ultimate ability to control malaria, reducing the ability of program planners to mobilize communities in malaria control.

Malaria-control programs. Malaria-control programs with health communication, learning theory, and community self-control components, however, have shown promise. A malaria control program in the Philippines (Amarillo, Lansang, Bilizario, Miguel, & Sepulveda, 1999) resulted in positive reception and (at least initial) behavior change. In villages in the southern Philippines, health workers posted "malarial monitoring boards," which mapped out the entire village: Each house in the village was represented and provided feedback as well as positive and negative reinforcement. Houses were color coded on a monthly basis. A blue code meant that the house had been entirely sprayed, green signified that the house was using insecticide-impregnated bed nets, yellow indicated that the house was using bed nets without insecticide, red meant that malaria had been diagnosed in someone in that house, and black related that a malaria death had occurred. After only 1 month of posting the malarial monitoring board, 60% of the residents in that village could identify what the board represented and were motivated to maintain their homes in the blue or green category.

A program to prevent deaths from malaria in Gambia had as its goal the distribution of bed nets dipped in insecticide through all primary health care sites. It included a nationwide media campaign and the involvement of campaign personnel and local health workers. The dipping process was arranged at the village compound level. Village chiefs, leaders of women's groups, and traditional birth attendants mobilized women in compounds to bring their bed nets for dipping on appointed days and not to wash the nets until the end of the rainy season. The cost for each life saved was $471 (mostly children under 5), and the cost per life year gained was $31.50 (Aikens et al., 1998). However, use of impregnated bed nets when the insecticide is sold may be as little as 20% of the use when treatment is offered for free. Primary health care services should include free insecticide to women with infants and small children, supplemented by sale through shops (Mueller, Cham, Jaffar, & Greenwood, 1997).

Dengue fever control. Also spread by the mosquito (*Aedes aegypti*) vector, dengue is one of the most prevalent diseases in the world, with two distinct forms: dengue, the most important re-emerging disease in the Americas, and dengue hemorrhagic fever, an emerging disease increasingly prevalent in tropical regions of the world. In general, the principal elements used to control *Aedes aegypti* have been insecticides and larvicides, such as malathion and temephos, depending at what point in the life cycle the intervention is targeted. Fish and turtles that eat larva can be placed in cisterns and other large containers, and the covering of these containers has also been promoted. Another control method involves source reduction through the organization of cleanup campaigns to get rid of unneeded containers. Unlike the Anopheles mosquito, the *Aedes aegypti* travels only short distances; therefore, these cleanup campaigns focus on household and neighborhood efforts. Recently, strategies that have promoted more efficient community participation have also been incorporated (Gubler, 1989).

A multicomponent dengue fever control effort in Honduras used some of the above and additional methods. The Honduran program emphasized *Aedes aegypti*-related eradication efforts, beginning with primary school children and extending all the way to individual households. At the household level, health promoters visited each individual owner or resident and discussed the danger of dengue fever and methods of its control. Because a large amount of mosquito egg development in Honduras occurred in outdoor concrete water-storage basins, the health promoter would demonstrate the *untadita* process: how to scrub the algae off the side of the water-storage containers to eliminate mosquito eggs and larva (Sherman et al., 1998). Individuals were asked to demonstrate their own understanding of the untadita and state whether they felt they would be able to carry out the procedure (for the aged or infirmed, assistance was procured from other sources). During subsequent revisits, the health promoter gave each individual feedback on whether progress had been made and verbally reinforced their accomplishments or gave them constructive criticism, had they not made sufficient progress. Although this effort was relatively labor-intensive, substantial improvement in the eradication of these breeding sites was achieved.

The Mérida (Yúcatan) Project formed part of a new approach for controlling dengue. Specifically, the Mérida effort sought to define mosquito production based on the presence of pupae in breeding sites; to identify the most frequent sites according to type, behavioral function, and classification as disposable or controllable; to identify the most effective and feasible practices in breeding-site control for adoption at the household level; and to design communication strategies to develop behavior-change interventions to promote the desired practices at the household level (Rivas & Lloyd, 1996).

A system that classified household containers as potential mosquito-breeding sites was designed for the project prior to developing control methods, based on the following categories: (a) disposable: those containers that were easier to eliminate because they were assumed to be trash; (b) controllable: containers to which the population assigned a behavioral function or value and that were not eliminated during garbage cleanup campaigns but that were susceptible to some kind of control, whether physical or chemical; and (c) controlled: those containers that by their condition cannot be mosquito-breeding sites.

Container function was defined as the use assigned by individuals to each container to satisfy their specific needs. Thus, if containers shared the same form and capacity (e.g., 10-liter plastic buckets) but had different behavioral functions (e.g., use in household cleaning versus drinking containers for animals) their potential control strategies would also differ (e.g., empty after use versus add lime to destroy mosquito eggs).

The complexity of large containers made of rough material (usually cement) made their care more difficult. Therefore, function was addressed within the context of type and volume of the container, as the latter determined complexity or simplicity of its care. Breeding sites were categorized into six different functions: water-storage containers, animal water dishes, aquatic plant containers, tires, containers having no use for the moment, and disposable containers. Once the functions of containers had been determined, some control actions were designed to prevent the development of pupae in them. The emphasis was not on preventing the container from being positive for larvae but to prevent larvae from reaching the pupal stage. For example, animal water dishes were to be washed and scrubbed once a week with a brush and detergent. Water-storage containers were to be washed and scrubbed once a week with a broom and detergent and to be emptied and allowed to dry for 6 hours twice per week. Lime was put into tires that could not be discarded.

Conclusions from pilot trials were that washing and scrubbing animal water dishes and flower vases required no major effort, pouring lime into tires was widely accepted, and washing and scrubbing water-storage containers was viewed as somewhat difficult.

Based on the formative research, several slogans were composed and pretested. The slogan enjoying the highest degree of acceptance was: "your family's peace of mind is close at hand—and is in your hands." This concept alluded to the role of the housewife, implying that it is neither difficult nor foreign for her to accomplish control.

The media mix for the promotion of control behaviors included radio and television, as well as the use of interpersonal communication through home visits and activities at the schools. Actions for controlling aquatic plants, flower vases, and larger containers used for storage (large tubs and drums) were communicated through household visits and school activities, as the interpersonal channel allowed for more detailed explanations of the control behaviors and permitted the message to be tailored to each household. The interpersonal communication aspect of the campaign began after some of the messages had already been broadcast over the air for some time, thus facilitating their identification by the target audience.

An average of 24 daily radio spots were broadcast for 5 months, and 14 weekly television spots were broadcast during a 5-month period. The mass media strategy called for the introduction of a new behavior each month, specific to animal water dishes, water-storage containers, tires, and not-in-use containers. Children in the fourth grade were targeted for special communication and control activities, and informative meetings with their mothers also were held. School activities motivated the children to transmit their knowledge of *Aedes aegypti* control to their mothers. Meetings with their mothers made them aware of the dengue problem and its potential to be controlled. The objective of the household visits was to establish direct contact with the target audience within their own environment for further explaining the control behaviors, adapting the messages according to the containers found, and carrying out a demonstration of the control actions.

Both interpersonal and mass media strategies resulted in an index reduction in animal water dishes, water storage containers, and tires, with a greater impact for interpersonal communication. However, full control of *Aedes aegypti* breeding sites was complicated not only by biological or climatic variables, but also by the functions of the containers as well as their size and structure. Animal water dishes were the most frequently found containers, followed by water-storage containers and tires. Control behavior before as well as after the campaign was higher for animal water dishes than for water-storage containers, due to the complexity of cleaning large, stationary objects.

Consistent with results from a previous effort in the Dominican Republic (Gordon, 1988), interpersonal communication via household visits was identified as being more influential than the mass media communication strategy, even though exposure was limited due to the brief intervention. As noted above, however, the mass media campaign may have "softened up" the target audience prior to the implementation of the apparently more effective interpersonal effort. Although the great majority of respondents still did not attempt to control tires, 13% at least mentioned that they put lime into their tires, indicating that it might be feasible for families to keep those containers under control. All houses that put lime into their tires showed an absence of larvae and pupae.

The Mérida evaluators concluded that achieving success in *Aedes aegypti* breeding-site control requires the identification of the most productive breeding sites, based on pupal productivity and the frequency with which these breeding sites are found in the environment. Before control behaviors are targeted, it is necessary to know the efficacy and feasibility of these behaviors (Rivas & Lloyd, 1996).

SUMMARY

Vaccine-preventable diseases, diarrhea, respiratory infections, and vector-borne diseases continue to play a major role in worldwide mortality, especially among children under 5 years old. Although smallpox has been eradicated worldwide and polio is on the verge of extinction, national and local immunization campaigns must be reinforced. Diarrhea kills primarily through dehydration, which can be effectively and inexpensively treated with oral rehydration solutions. Respiratory infections require vigilant parents who detect early signs of pneumonia in their children, and an effective health care system must provide appropriate treatment. Control strategies for vector-borne diseases will vary depending on the type of vector, but these may involve eliminating the vector, minimizing contact between the vector and humans, responding rapidly to the illness, and/or isolating the stricken patient until the threat of spreading the disease has passed.

FURTHER READING

Cutts, F. T. (1998). Advances and challenges for the expanded programme on immunization. *British Medical Bulletin, 54*(2), 445-461.

Graeff, J., Elder, J., & Booth, E. (1993). *Communications for health behavior change: A developing country perspective.* San Francisco: Jossey-Bass.

Hinman, A. (1999). Eradication of vaccine-preventable diseases. *Annual Review of Public Health, 20,* 211-229.

▒ Note

1. The Plasmodium parasite matures and reproduces in the mosquito, thereby making it the parasite's definitive host, whereas human beings are the parasite's intermediate host (Negerá et al., 1993).

6

HIV/AIDS

The role of human behavior in the transmission of infectious diseases has never been clearer than since the outbreak of the AIDS epidemic two decades ago. Initially thinking that AIDS affected male homosexual communities almost exclusively,[1] epidemiologists zeroed in on the role of specific high-risk behaviors, such as frequent changes of sexual partners and unprotected anal intercourse (Anderson, 1992). Initially, it was even assumed that HIV infections would remain contained within the gay community. The epidemic, however, soon came to affect people of all ages and sexual orientations. Today, HIV infections worldwide result primarily from heterosexual contact, injection drug use (IDU), and mother-to-infant (vertical) transmission (Fauci, 1999; UNAIDS/WHO, 1999), although this varies substantially by region and nation. For example, South Africa estimates that 79% of its AIDS cases are due to heterosexual transmission, 7% due to homosexual contact, 13% due to vertical transmission, and 1% due to transfusions, whereas Gambia reports 93% due to heterosexual contact and nearly all the rest due to vertical transmission. Data from the Dominican Republic show

6%, 5%, 4%, and 4% of AIDS cases caused by heterosexual and homosexual contact, IDU, transfusions, and vertical transmission, respectively, whereas these figures were 18%, 48%, 32%, 1%, and 1% for the United States. The American pattern is similar to that in most Western countries. In Eastern Europe, cases are more likely to be due to IDU, whereas Romania indicates that one third of its AIDS cases are caused by the transfusion of contaminated blood. Myanmar (Burma) indicates that nearly two thirds of its AIDS cases are due to heterosexual contact and nearly all of the rest due to IDU, whereas neighboring Thailand reports 89% due to heterosexual contact and nearly all of the rest equally divided between IDU and vertical transmission (UNAIDS/WHO, 1999). Regardless of the cause, unlike many other infectious diseases, AIDS is almost entirely preventable (Fauci, 1999).

Although some progress in preventing the disease has recently been realized in industrialized countries (e.g., Sikkema et al., 2000), the global death toll from AIDS is currently about 2.6 million per year. In sub-Saharan African nations alone, there were an astounding 2.2 million deaths from AIDS in 1998 (85% of the world's total), a rate that is accelerating. Already, Africa has lost more than 14 million people to AIDS ("Africa AIDS crisis," 2000). The ensuing fallout has left an even more vexing problem: Over 10 million children under the age of 14 have been made orphans (contrasted to 13 million orphans throughout Europe after the total devastation of World War II) (Batholet, 2000). This figure could increase to an incredible 40 million by 2010 (Africa AIDS crisis, 2000). The proliferation of orphans portends problems for decades to come: These children will likely be illiterate and will turn to illegal activities to survive. Because such activities typically include prostitution,[2] these secondary AIDS victims themselves are likely to be compelled to work as sex workers or even to be enslaved to this work, thus perpetuating—and eventually dying from—the epidemic (Masland & Nordland, 2000). Countries that are already economically crippled will have to cope not only with this ever-increasing dependent population but also with the fact that a disproportionate number of AIDS victims are among their educated elite—doctors, nurses, and teachers.

As with so many other diseases, children and women are increasingly the victims of AIDS. The most brutal symptom of the exploitation of and violence against women involves the trafficking in females as young as 8 years old, as men—usually fathers or other male relatives—sell girls to agents of the sex industry. Asia especially is ripe for this despicable commerce, with estimates of women and children trafficked each year from the tens of thousands to the millions (Bennett, 1999). Trafficking is generally for the purposes of prostitution and, therefore, is part and parcel of the growing AIDS epidemic, as many prostitutes are forced by their clients to have unprotected sex or are paid more for forgoing condom use. Nevertheless, forced child labor is also often the end result of this trafficking. The term may be narrowly defined as a form of kidnaping and enslavement, although broader definitions such as that of the President's Interagency Council on Women may be more appropriate:

> All acts involved in the recruitment, transport, harboring or sale of persons within national or across international borders through deception or fraud, coercion or force, or debt bondage for purposes of placing persons in situations of forced labor or services, such as forced prostitution or sexual services, domestic servitude, or other forms of slavery-like practices. (Bennett, 1999, p. 9)

Prostitution is, by no means, the only direct source of HIV infection, however. Not knowing their husband's HIV status, many wives become infected. For example, Baingana, Choi, Barrett, Byansi, and Hearst (1995) conducted a cross-sectional survey in the New Mulago Hospital in Kampala, Uganda, among women partners of male AIDS patients admitted to medical wards. Only 12% knew of their partner's AIDS diagnosis. More than half of the women affirmed the desirability of HIV testing, although few (5%) had been tested. Those who stated the need for HIV testing were in a newer relationship, had fewer children, and were more financially independent of their husbands.

Should infected women become pregnant and decide to carry the pregnancy to term, there is a high probability of passing the disease on to their children. In developing countries, pediatric AIDS accounts for 15% to 20% of all AIDS cases (Srison et al., 1995). Women who are abstaining from sex during the postnatal recuperation period may encounter an increased probability that their husbands will seek extramarital partners without using condoms, as was documented by Cleland, Ali, and Capo-Chichi (1999) in a study in Benin (West Africa), placing both partners at risk of sexually transmitted diseases (STDs)/HIV infection. Rather than advocating empowerment to lower the risk of these women, the authors conclude that "family planning practitioners in this region should not hesitate to recommend the early resumption of sex and suitable methods of postpartum contraception for women who express concern or uncertainty about their husband's behaviour" (p. 125). This recommendation stands in stark contrast to the argument presented by Zierler and Krieger (1997), who examine HIV infection among women within the framework of feminism, the social production of disease, ecosocial conditions, and human rights. Specifically, they advise researchers working in this area to examine, among other things, how gender and social and economic inequalities affect the health of women, especially as applied to HIV infections. For example, they note that a woman may be reluctant to have sex with her male partner due to his refusal to wear a condom but will do so anyway because she fears losing whatever material support he provides her (and her children) or even because he may become violent when she asks him to use a condom. The latter fear is far greater among women sex workers when having sex with clients compared to nonclients (Lurie, Fernandes, Hughes, Arevalo, & Hudes, 1995). Loss of support and domestic violence are, in turn, obvious precursors of homelessness, which puts women at higher risk through IV drug use or the need to turn to prostitution for income.

Although the world is finally becoming aware of the scope of the HIV/AIDS problem, with the exception of those in South Africa and Uganda, African leaders have been slow to address it: Not a single one of them attended a recent international AIDS conference in Lusaka, Zambia (Batholet, 2000). Such reluctance is likely the combined product of denial, prejudice, and fear of economic loss due to less tourism.

Interventions

Soderlund, Lavis, Broomberg, and Mills (1993) and others have outlined the basic prevention strategies for HIV infections, among which are the following:

1. Using mass media to promote safer sex, including teaching essential facts about HIV transmission and reducing discrimination against AIDS victims. This may be targeted toward the general public, such as public school children, rather than specific high-risk populations.

2. Promoting safer sex interpersonally, usually targeting highly vulnerable groups. For example, in a study of adults in Zimbabwe, better knowledge and practice were associated with levels of education, religion, travel, and media exposure; personal risk perception was higher among those with more media exposure and contact with medical services. But many AIDS victims, because of poverty, migration due to work or regional conflict, or other factors have no access to mainstream interventions or media. Intensive interpersonal communication/peer education campaigns are needed to reach those without access to modern media and at highest risk (Gregson, Zhuwau, Anderson, & Chandiwana, 1997).

3. Using social marketing to promote condom use.

4. Preventing unsafe drug use among intravenous drug users, at least among those who are not involved in substance abuse treatment programs. This intervention consists of education about the need to eliminate needle sharing and ways to disinfect needles, as well as bleach distribution and needle exchange.

5. Expanding prevention and treatment services for STDs, which would not only improve the general health status of the population but reduce the risk of HIV infections as well.

6. Conducting careful screening of donated blood and disposing of infected blood to maintain a healthy blood supply.

7. Preventing the vertical transmission of AIDS through antiretroviral interventions and possibly the substitution of formula feeding for breast-feeding among infected mothers (Soderlund, Zwi, Kinghorn, & Gray, 1999).[3]

8. Continuing the development, testing, and promotion of other methods for preventing HIV transmission, such as microbicides for application in the vagina before sexual intercourse and the female condom, as Fauci (1999) and others have urged.

Specific examples of programs addressing these and related issues are presented below.

Community Self-Control

Convincing communities to take charge of preventing the spread of HIV has proven slow work, probably due to the strong stigma attached to people with AIDS and the behaviors that put individuals at risk for the infection. Therefore, communities of at-risk people have had to define themselves as such and begin to combat the spread of the infection among themselves. The gay communities in the San Francisco Bay area and elsewhere took responsibility for promoting safer sex among themselves and for pressuring public health and political officials for more aggressive efforts and better funding for research and treatment. In addition, groups of sex workers have begun to organize themselves for mutual education and protection. For example, in Mykolaiv, Ukraine, the Charity Foundation organization recruits current and former sex workers to educate their peers, pass out condoms, discuss strategies for ensuring that their clients use them, and prevent one another from being beaten by their clients or pimps (Hyde, 1999).

Dealing with the problem of selling women and girls into prostitution requires three categories of action: preventing women and children from being trafficked in the first place, protecting and assisting victims of trafficking, and prosecuting traffickers and enforcing laws against trafficking. A novel approach to community-level interpersonal communication to promote self-control has been implemented by the Maiti Nepal program, which helps women who have been sold into prostitution in India to find their way home and become reintegrated into communal Nepali culture. In a form of face-to-face media advocacy, program representatives meet with village chiefs and parents to prevent trafficking, as well, exposing them to the stark reality of life for these girls, once they arrive in India, and exposing the lies traffickers may tell (Bennett, 1999).

An important aspect of AIDS prevention is ensuring the overall reproductive health of adolescents. In Lusaka, Zambia, community input was used to promote the installation of Youth Corners in clinics, private spaces accessed separately from the primary outpatient waiting room. Ten adolescent peer counselors, selected via community recommendations, staffed the Youth Corners, which were initially housed in two of seven target clinics. These peer counselors received intensive initial training, booster training to share their experiences and to self-generate solutions to problems, and monetary supplements for transportation and miscellaneous costs. Billboards throughout the city indicated the availability of the Youth Corners services, and posters on clinics pointed out their participation in the program as well as the location of the private entrance. One subgroup of counselors took it on themselves to obtain access to a vacant building, which they used as a performing arts center with an HIV-prevention theme. Youth clubs and schools invited the counselors to give talks on reproductive health and describe the Youth Corners services. After 15 months, the counselors had met with 12,372 young women and 5,845 young men in individual and group sessions. They distributed 42,814 condoms and 14,587 foaming tablet spermicides. After observing the success of and client satisfaction with the Youth Corners, a third clinic requested funding to establish such a service (Newton, 2000, pp. 24-32).

Health Communication

Health communication has been relied on extensively for the prevention of HIV/AIDS and the promotion of family planning (see the Rogers et al., 1999, Tanzania example, pp. 58-59), with a variety of safe-sex or related messages being communicated aggressively or subtly through electronic, print, and interpersonal media. Sex workers have been given supplies of condoms and training on condom-negotiation skills, for instance, how they can skillfully convince their clientele to wear condoms and protect both of them from STDs. For example, Bhave and colleagues (1995) developed an HIV intervention targeting sex workers and madams in the brothels of Bombay. In a controlled intervention trial, with measurements before and after the intervention, 334 sex workers and 20 madams were recruited from an intervention site, and 207 and 17, respectively, from a control site in red-light areas of Bombay. Subjects in the intervention group underwent a 6-month program of educational videos, small-group discussions, and pictorial educational materials; free condoms were also distributed. Baseline levels of knowledge about HIV and experience with condoms were extremely low among both sex workers and madams. The baseline prevalence of HIV antibodies was 47% in the intervention group and 41% in the control group. After the intervention, however, the incidence rates for HIV and STDs were significantly different in the two groups, at 0.05 and 0.16 per person-year of follow-up for HIV, 0.08 and 0.22 per person-year for antibodies to syphilis, and 0.04 and 0.12 per person-year for hepatitis B surface antigen in the intervention and control women, respectively. Following the intervention, women reported increased levels of condom use, and 41% said they were willing to refuse clients who would not use them. However, both the sex workers and the madams were concerned about losing business if condom use was required. The authors concluded that successful interventions can be developed for these women, and even a partial increase in condom use may decrease the transmission of HIV and STDs. Intervention programs of longer duration that target madams and clients and make condoms easily available are urgently needed at multiple sites in red-light areas.

Visrutaratna, Lindan, Sirhorachai, and Mandel (1995) developed and evaluated a multifaceted AIDS prevention program relying heavily on vicarious and direct reinforcement to increase condom use among sex workers in the city of Chiang Mai, Thailand. Their year-long intervention targeted sex workers, brothel owners, and clients, promoted cooperation among these groups and the public health office, and established a free condom supply for sex establishments. Nearly 500 women from 43 establishments took part in the program, encompassing nearly all direct sex workers in urban Chiang Mai. The intervention included repeated small-group training sessions for sex workers, in which experienced women (whom they called superstars) acted as peer educators. The official designation of model brothel encouraged all brothel owners in Chiang Mai to insist on use of condoms by sex workers and to encourage clients to use condoms. In a clever approach to the evaluation of this program, specially trained volunteers posing as clients tested a subsample of sex workers to see whether they insisted on condom use. The intervention was well received by sex workers and garnered support and cooperation from brothel owners. Before the intervention, only 42% of women surveyed by volunteers posing as clients refused to have sex without a condom, when the client insisted and offered to pay three times the usual fee. Following the program, 92% refused; 1 year later, although this figure had leveled off to 78%, refusal was still nearly twice that of baseline.

Voluntary counseling and testing is a key component of many HIV intervention efforts, which rely on competent face-to-face interaction between primary health care workers and patients. Pretest counseling is especially central to the prevention of vertical transmission of HIV, as many pregnant women have no idea that they have been infected and need to be encouraged to be tested. Cartoux et al. (1999) compared individual and small-group pretest counseling in two prenatal clinics in Burkina Faso. Of the 3,031 women receiving individual counseling, 93.3% accepted the test, compared to 89.4% of the 927 receiving group counseling. Knowledge change favored the group intervention. The authors conclude that group pretest counseling for pregnant women may have a superior public health impact if implemented systematically.

Other health communications efforts have been less promising. For example, Aplasca and colleagues (1995) developed a school-based AIDS education program for public high schools in a semi-urban district of metropolitan Manila, in the Philippines. The teacher-led AIDS program was designed to provide students with accurate information about AIDS, particularly to dispel misconceptions about casual contagion, foster positive attitudes toward people with AIDS, and develop skills aimed at clarifying values and assessing intended behavior. At baseline, 11% of students (20% of males and 4% of females) reported ever having had sexual intercourse (mean age 14 years). Among these, condom use was at 24%. At posttest, significant effects favoring the intervention group were observed in knowledge and attitudes toward people with AIDS. There was no statistically significant overall effect on intended preventive behavior. However, the program appeared to delay the students' intended onset of sexual activity.

Condom Provision and Communication

The simple provision of condoms has been a cornerstone of many HIV/AIDS prevention programs. Thailand's public health strategy, for example, consists of three components: providing a continuous supply of free condoms to commercial sex establishments and to female sex workers at the point of their STD medical checkups; promoting universal condom use in commercial sex and identifying commercial sex establishments used by men who have been treated for STDs for stricter compliance; and supporting this with a mass media campaign using television and radio to promote the general reduction of high-risk behavior, such as avoiding commercial sex altogether. This strategy appears to be paying off; for example, Thai military men demonstrated an 80% reduction in HIV incidence between 1991-1993 and 1994-1995 (Celentano et al., 1998).

Other research has suggested new directions for HIV/AIDS prevention among adolescents. In a study of HIV/AIDS-related anxieties associated with HIV prevention in adolescents in Nigeria, Kenya, and Zimbabwe, Venier, Ross, and Akande (1997) found four major HIV/AIDS-related factors underlying an extensive list of psychosocial questionnaire items. The investigators labeled these factors as *condom interactions, refusal of risk, confiding in significant others,* and *contact with people with HIV/AIDS.* Examples of items pertaining to each category are as follows:

> *Condom interactions:* Going into a pharmacy and asking to buy condoms, carrying condoms in a wallet or handbag, asking a friend to borrow one, buying condoms off the shelf, starting a social conversation about condom use
>
> *Refusal of risk:* Telling someone who has had multiple sex partners that you don't want to have sex with him/her, telling close friends that you won't share needles, telling a casual friend that you don't want to have sex at the present, telling an IV drug user that you don't want to have sex, refusing to have sex without a condom being used
>
> *Confiding in significant others:* Telling parents that you have an STD, telling your boy/girlfriend that you have an STD, going to a clinic for an STD or HIV test, phoning the STD/AIDS hotline, seeking help for IV drug use
>
> *Hugging or visiting a friend or relative who has HIV or AIDS.*

The authors suggest that HIV prevention efforts should focus on these target areas of social anxieties rather than just on HIV/AIDS-related facts.

SUMMARY

Currently, about 2.6 million people die from AIDS every year, a number that continues to grow rapidly. About 10 million children in Africa alone have been made orphans by AIDS. Although some programs in wealthier nations have realized success, the epidemic continues to devastate Africa and is spreading rapidly in Asia. Crowley (2000) and others have outlined four basic issues that must be addressed if the epidemic is to be controlled:

Break the silence. First, the world, and particularly the nations most affected by AIDS, must admit the reality and scope of the problem. The stigma associated with AIDS and the fear of a loss of prestige and income (e.g., through reductions in tourism) have discouraged leaders from speaking out. This appears to be changing, at least in those nations most affected by the epidemic.

Promote safer sex. Broad-based health communication, social marketing, learning theory, media advocacy, and community self-control methods must be applied vigorously and tailored to each culture. Clinic-based and other face-to-face programs that provide basic risk education, promote risk-reduction attitudes and skills (such as condom use and condom negotiation), and reinforce progress toward behavior change in these areas have been shown to be effective (Sikkema et al., 2000). All communication efforts must carefully avoid victim-blaming, especially with respect to the topic of prostitution.

Empower women. Women currently account for more than half of new AIDS cases, with infection rates among teenage girls five times that among boys. Assertiveness about partner's condom use may be effective in some cases, but men generally hold the upper hand and may even be willing to pay more for unprotected sex. Progress in the development of affordable microbicides and the female condom is urgently needed. Generally, however, cultures that subordinate and victimize women will place them at high risk for illness and early death.

Develop and use vaccines. Lesions caused by gonorrhea, chlamydia, and other STDs greatly increase the chances of HIV transmission. Inexpensive vaccines to treat STDs in general are needed. More critical, however, is a preventive vaccine for HIV, which is in the early stages of development. Only $300 million per year is being spent on vaccine research worldwide.

FURTHER READING

The reader is advised to keep abreast of rapid developments in the control of HIV/AIDS through journals such as *AIDS* and *International Journal of STDs and AIDS.*

▨ Notes

1. Hence, initially labeled GRIDs (Gay Related Infectious Diseases).

2. There is even a widespread belief that having sex with a virgin girl will cure AIDS (Masland & Nordland, 2000), thus increasing the demand for child prostitutes.

3. In spite of the beneficial effects of antiretroviral therapy for HIV-infected people themselves, many are not responsive to the therapy, cannot tolerate the side effects, or have trouble maintaining compliance. Moreover, the virus persists in sanctuaries not reachable by the drug (Fauci, 1999, p. 1048). Given these problems and the enormous expense of the therapy, it is unlikely to become a public health tool for the foreseeable future, and certainly not in developing countries.

7

Tobacco Control

The tobacco epidemic has taken many ironic turns in its deadly 500-year journey across the public health landscape. When Columbus first set foot in the New World, many members of his crew saw natives smoking crudely rolled tobacco or pipes made from plant material. Columbus later reported this substance to be a favorite of Indian medicine men, as tobacco smoke produced visions and gave the Indians powers to predict the future (Cortés & Elder, 2000). The Spanish missionary Romano Pane sent Emperor Carlos V tobacco seeds in 1518, which resulted in the first cultivation of tobacco in Europe. Although tobacco was suppressed by the Inquisition (as only Satan would confer on humans the ability to blow smoke from their mouths), the substance had begun to conquer its third continent (Escohotado, 1998).

By the end of the 16th century, scores of sailors and soldiers were returning to Europe with the tobacco habit. Smoking was still proscribed in many societies, with penalties as severe as decapitation in the Ottoman Empire for smoking's violation of the precepts of the Koran. Tobacco consumption, therefore, frequently took the form of snuff inhaled into the nose, a practice that was adopted quickly by European nobility (Braudel, 1984). The commercial cultivation of tobacco began in 1612 by English colonist John Roye, who correctly identified ideal soil and climate conditions offered by his colony of Virginia. This profitable crop rapidly spread throughout the English colonies and, along with cotton, eventually provided America the economic wherewithal to revolt against England (Cortés & Elder, 2000). Smoking slowly spread throughout the Americas, Europe, and Asia until the early 20th century, with the development of the rolled cigarette. World War II saw a rapid spread of smoking, with American soldiers and sailors receiving daily rations of cigarettes free or at a very low cost.

Until recently, tobacco could be seen as the revenge of American natives for the loss of their lands, languages, and lives: At least, they had given the conquering Caucasians the literal seeds of their destruction, as tobacco eventually became the biggest killer of populations in industrialized countries. For much of this time, tobacco producers were, indeed, satisfied with the profits realized by selling to "their own kind." Eventually, however, American, British, and other tobacco companies sought to replace Caucasian smokers who quit or perished from their habit by marketing in less developed countries. The invention of the cigarette machine a century ago stimulated tobacco industry interest in large, new markets. After its invention, James Duke, the founder of British American Tobacco, is reported to have examined an atlas and said, "China: 430 million. That is where we are going to sell cigarettes" (Dobson, 1946, cited in MacKay & Crofton, 1996). Today, over half of the world's smokers are in Asia, a proportion that continues to grow (MacKay & Crofton, 1996). Thus, the plants brought to Europe by Columbus, Raleigh, and others are back on boats, redirected (both legally and via smuggling) to vulnerable populations in poorer regions of the world.

The Epidemiological Picture Today

Today, nearly a third of the world's adult population smokes, producing more than 10,000 deaths per day (Hurst, 1999). Of these more than 1 billion smokers, one third are Chinese citizens. Nearly 3 million people die of tobacco-related causes per year in economically developed countries alone, half of them before the age of 70 (Wald & Hackshaw, 1996). This figure approaches 1 million per year in developing countries, including China (Peto et al., 1996).

Developing countries and former socialist nations vary substantially with respect to their stage of awareness and action regarding most tobacco control. At the basic level is Africa, where, although smoking is being adopted widely, few of even the most fundamental facts are known about its health effects (Asma &

Pederson, 1999). More males (50%-60%) but fewer females (2%-10%) smoke in developing countries (MacKay & Crofton, 1996). In 1990, tobacco was responsible for 24% of male and 7% of female deaths in developed countries, contrasted to 40% of male and 17% of female deaths in the countries of the former Soviet Union and Soviet bloc (Peto et al., 1996). At least eight types of cancer are products of smoking, with lung cancer nearly exclusively linked to the habit. Six other potentially fatal diseases may be partially or entirely caused by smoking, including respiratory and ischemic heart diseases, chronic obstructive lung disease, stroke, and pneumonia. About 250 million children and adolescents who are currently experimenting with tobacco will someday die from it. By 2030, tobacco use will be the world's greatest killer (Hurst, 1999), with as many as 10 million dying annually from its use (Peto et al., 1996). About 7 million of these will be in developing countries (MacKay & Crofton, 1996).

The former Soviet bloc countries and the newly independent states formerly comprising the Soviet Union offer a fertile marketing target for American and multinational tobacco companies. Although more out of concern for preventing the loss of hard currency than for the public's health, pre-1990, state-owned tobacco monopolies prevented imports from multinational tobacco companies and the accompanying aggressive marketing campaigns (Chapman, 1994). For example, in Bulgaria, only 5% of men and fewer than 1% of women over 70 years of age smoke, whereas 58% of men and 30% of women ages 30 to 39 do so (Balabanova, Bobak, & McKee, 1998). In Russia, smoking already accounts for 30% of all male deaths. A survey of 1,587 Russians showed smoking to be common among males of all ages, with prevalence rates of 65% and 73% among men ages 18 to 24 and 25 to 34. As in Bulgaria, however, women have only recently taken up the habit, with 28% of those 18 to 34 versus only 5% of those 55 and older identifying themselves as current smokers (McKee et al., 1998).

Recent surveys offer good news not only for multinational but also for domestic tobacco producers around the world. In Ankara, Turkey, a survey of 1,093 children ages 7 to 13 years showed logo recognition proportions of 83%, 93%, and 73% for Samsun (a Turkish brand), Camel, and Marlboro, respectively, favorably compared to Cheetos (59%), McDonald's (67%), and Coca Cola (89%) (Emri, Bagci, Karakoca, & Baris, 1998).

Environmental and Economic Impact

Harming indigenous societies and the habitat. By 1985, 73% of the world's tobacco was grown in developing countries, but 63% of these countries were still spending more on importing tobacco than what they earned exporting it (MacKay

& Crofton, 1996). Multinational organizations not directly connected to the tobacco industry may still have an impact on the tobacco economy and culture of developing countries. In the 1970s, the World Bank sponsored wider cultivation of tobacco through financing and providing expertise as a means to assist developing-country economies. In Tanzania alone, the number of tobacco farmers increased from 6,070 in 1970 to 25,880 in 1978, with the area under cultivation more than doubling in this same time period (Waluye, 1994). The economies of Zimbabwe and Malawi now depend on tobacco exports (Asma & Pederson, 1999).

The environmental and economic impact of this transition has been enormous, with farmers now required to travel 10 km or more to forests to obtain firewood for curing their crops; the clearing of forest areas for additional tobacco planting has accelerated. The natural forest cover of the West Nile region of Uganda, for example, has been reduced by more than half in recent decades for additional tobacco cultivation and firewood (Muwanga-Bayego, 1994). While farm families have remained poor, larger portions of their land are being devoted to tobacco at the expense of millet, cassava, and other food crops. Women and children often have to spend their time working the expanding tobacco fields, at the expense of child care and schooling.[1]

The Marlboro Man has positioned himself as America's top businessman in West African countries such as Senegal, as well as throughout the world, exploiting youthful fascination with the United States through ubiquitous "Come to Marlboro Country" billboards (White, 1998).

In West African countries, as well as in more socially conservative countries such as Indonesia, sexily clad and heavily made-up women offer free samples of Marlboro and other brands to male patrons and passersby.

Smuggling. Although immoral, most of the above activities do not violate national or international laws. Yet, increasing numbers of cigarettes sold on the international market are marketed illegally. Joossens (2000) has shown that this figure has reached 6% worldwide and is as high as 13% in Eastern Europe, 12% in Africa and the Middle East, and 9% in Latin America. Smuggling has traditionally been linked to bootlegging, efforts by individuals or small gangs to bring thousands of cigarettes at a time across a border from where they are legally less expensive (i.e., where taxes are lower) to where they cost more. Such activity is at least indirectly encouraged by the tobacco industry. For example, British American Tobacco (BAT) exports billions of cigarettes to Andorra, a mountainous resort country located on the Spanish-French border whose own population is only 63,000.

Increasingly, however, smuggling occurs on a much grander scale (in so-called container smuggling), with hundreds of thousands of cigarettes being

This Panama City Marlboro ad belittles a public health admonition to "Say No to Drugs."

transported without duties in ship and airplane containers. Although such smuggling is often the domain of organized crime, internal documents from the BAT and RJR transhipment of cigarettes to Canada via Aruba and Puerto Rico have demonstrated industry support for this effort as well. In the United Kingdom, it is estimated that 80% of duty-not-paid (DNP) cigarettes come via container smuggling (Joossens, 2000).

Smuggling relies on informal distribution networks (from container shipments to street selling) and a lack of enforcement of existing laws that require tax stamps. Smuggling not only promotes consumption by providing cheaper cigarettes but also results in the sale of cigarettes with no health warnings and increases the pressure on governments to reduce cigarette taxes (as was the case in Canada in the early 1990s).

Tobacco-Control Interventions

For more than a half century, cigarette smoking has been recognized as a major killer of populations of developed countries. Gradually, a broad array of learning-theory-based procedures, health communications, community activism, media advocacy, and policy interventions have taken on this tobacco problem, resulting in a gradual rollback of the epidemic in the West. For decades, the emphasis was on expensive smoking-cessation programs, including both nicotine-fading and satiation approaches. When these programs were accompanied by nicotine replacement therapy (e.g., nicotine patches), they gradually began to show some promise, although this substantially increased their expensiveness. Somewhat later, recognizing the futility of trying to get people to withdraw from an established addiction, especially hard-core smokers (Emery, Gilpin, Ake, Farkas, & Pierce, 2000), programs shifted their attention to the prevention of first-time or regular smoking. These programs specifically addressed peer pressure to begin smoking and interpersonal skills designed to counteract this pressure. Again, the bulkiness (e.g., requiring 10 to 20 classroom hours over 2 or more school years) and limited effectiveness of many prevention programs have limited their widespread adoption.

Over time, tobacco-control experts sought more aggressive and accessible methods to promote tobacco control. Mass media spots to counter the tobacco industry image, taken off the airways as part of an American congressional compromise with the industry 30 years ago, once again came into vogue. These spots aimed not only to encourage prevention and cessation but also to question the legitimacy of the tobacco industry and its marketing. Mass media interventions have helped lower smoking initiation in the United States (Siegel & Biener, 2000; Worden et al., 1996; see also http://www.state.fl.us/tobacco/ca0000.htm) and northern Europe. Provocative themes and messages may be especially attractive to adolescents and may boost the preventive power of such spots (Hafstad et al., 1997).

Policy interventions, first ignored by legislators who feared the industry's power or benefitted from its generous campaign support, have gradually gained favor. Cigarette machines, smoking in public buildings and at worksites, and other tobacco culture mainstays are slowly being legislated out of existence in the United States and elsewhere, and the enforcement of existing ordinances (e.g., ban of sales of individual cigarettes or to minors) is taken more seriously.[2] France and other countries have taken the lead in banning or strictly limiting tobacco advertising. Lawsuits initiated by individuals and later by states resulted in tacit admission by the industry of its liability in the deaths of millions and settlements of extraordinary sums of money. Media advocacy has mobilized public opinion to support these more aggressive actions, while community activists (e.g., DOC [Doctors Ought to Care] or the "Bugga Up" campaign in Australia) have con-

TABLE 7.1 Summary of Tobacco-Control Experiences in Developed Countries

Interventions	Efficacy	Cost-Effectiveness	Reach	Advantages and Disadvantages
Smoking cessation contests	Modest (5%–15% range)	Very high—large number of smokers may sign up and receive prizes that are often donated by community	Very high if backed by good media	Cessation generally is noncontroversial. However, addiction may already be firmly in place, making relapse rates very high
Telephone quit lines	6-month cessation rates at up to 20%	Moderate	Very good if backed by media and calls are toll free	See above; such programs require well-staffed phones and language-appropriate operators
Physician advice	5% range	Very cost-effective	Modest	Physicians seem easily discouraged; reimbursement for counseling is limited
Nicotine replacement therapy	Results range above 30% if backed by counseling program	Price of prescription patches may deter some smokers	Can be high, especially with private marketing efforts	May be needed with highly addicted smokers. Some danger if smoker is concurrently using other forms of tobacco
Standard stop-smoking clinics	Low cessation rates	Costly to staff	Low	Only recommended in conjunction with other methods

TABLE 7.1 (*continued*)

		Efficacy	Cost-Effectiveness	Reach	Advantages and Disadvantages
Prevention Approaches	School or other organizationally based programs	Long-term prevention effects have been as high as 50%	Require considerable teacher as well as classroom time	Modest to low, depending on peer versus teacher training models	Prevention programs are generally supported by the public; even the industry gives them lip service. Published views have generally shown disappointing results and reluctance of schools to incorporate aggressive programs
Mass media	Examples: California's media campaign sponsored by tobacco tax revenues	Low prevention or cessation rates	Media pieces should be professionally produced and air time purchased; ads must be changed frequently	Extremely high reach	Aggressive spots can be controversial but may be quite effective, especially as part of an overall tobacco-control effort supporting not only behavior but also policy change
Policy	Clean Indoor Air Acts	Not only protects nonsmokers but encourages smokers to quit	Political and legal battles may be lengthy	Can be extremely high, especially with large work or public places	Important cornerstone in establishing a smoke-free society
	Health warnings on tobacco packaging	Possibly some background influence	No cost	Reaches all tobacco consumers	Same as above; eventually ignored by habitual user

TABLE 7.1 (continued)

Sales limitations	Banning sales to teens and enforcing bans considered a "must" in preventing uptake		Enforcement (e.g., via "sting operations") required of local or regional government	Reaches all adolescent consumers; if ban extends to all vending machines, this may impact adult smoking as well	Non-controversial in comparison with other policy initiatives
	Tax increases	Elasticity of .5 or higher	None (except for lobbying)	Not only reduces quantity and even prevalence of smoking but also raises revenue that can fund additional efforts	Will be resisted by tobacco interests, but an extremely effective approach
Media advocacy and community activism	Signature-gathering effort to place tobacco control initiatives on ballots	Goal is to challenge legitimacy and legality of tobacco industry and its tactics, not to directly promote prevention or cessation	Inexpensive if carried out by volunteer activists and if free news coverage is achieved	Good reach if highly controversial activity or media piece receives widespread coverage	Relies on cadre of activists working in relatively liberal political environment

SOURCE: Adapted from Reid, 1996, and Elder et al., 1994.

fronted the industry directly through demonstrations, disruptions of industry events, and even defacement of billboard advertising.

Table 7.1 summarizes tobacco-control experiences in Western countries in terms of cessation, prevention, mass media, policy, and media advocacy interventions.

Ironically, some of the same wealthy countries whose people have benefitted from aggressive tobacco control at home have aggressively tried to sell the substance elsewhere. Thailand provides an excellent case example from the late 1980s. In 1985, American and transnational companies began advertising on Thai billboards, mocking an advertising ban in existence at that time. Imported cigarettes were still illegal, but the Americans were counting on the General Agreement on Tariffs and Trade (GATT) board to rule against this restriction. Angered by these actions, antismoking activists in Thailand gathered 6 million signatures in 1987 supporting anti-tobacco policies. Nevertheless, GATT sided with the tobacco companies, and imports began in 1992.

Price cutting, illegal advertising, and other cynical promotions continued, in which the pro-tobacco forces far outspent the modest tobacco control efforts of largely voluntary agencies. However, the Thai people and politicians gradually sympathized with the plight of the activists, and changes again were realized. Legislation controlling the sale of tobacco and protecting nonsmokers was passed; the Sports Commission prohibited tobacco industry sponsorship of sports events; taxes on cigarettes were raised twice in 5 years, to 71.5% of the retail price; and health warnings now cover 30% of the package. Lively anti-tobacco ads are appearing in many forms and outlets. In all, these efforts have resulted in a drop of male smoking prevalence from 49% to 38% between 1986 and 1999, and female prevalence declined from 4.1% to 2.4% during this same period (Vateesatokit, Hughes, & Ritthphakdee, 2000). Even where they are outgunned, persistent public health efforts at the societal level can result in important progress.

SUMMARY

Finally being brought under control in the industrialized world, the tobacco epidemic is spreading rapidly throughout Asia, Africa, and elsewhere. Strategies for tobacco control have taken an increasingly more aggressive tone to match the marketing practices of the tobacco industry.

The individual contributions of any one strategy are difficult to discern. However, general results of tobacco-control experiences, as presented in Table 7.1, show us that there is probably no need to repeat the entire spectrum of tobacco-control activities in developing countries, which can scarcely afford basic primary care services, let alone nicotine patches and hours of refusal skill role-playing among all public school children. We now are all aware of what does and does not work. Policy and media interventions should now become the tobacco-control methods of choice throughout the world.

Reflecting this more aggressive stance, an international panel of tobacco-control experts developed a set of generic recommendations applicable to all countries, regardless of their state of economic development (Samet, Yach, Taylor, & Becker, 1998). Among their recommendations were the following:

1. Tobacco control action should be organized outside of the government, reducing the conflict of interest that government officials may have due to tax revenues from tobacco sales. Government need for revenue has often guided tobacco taxation and trading policies, at the expense of public health (Chapman, 1994).

2. Smuggling needs to be stopped. This can be done by restricting sales to official tobacco outlets, placing prominent tax stamps on packages, making labels clearer (e.g., with country-specific health warnings), increasing penalties for smuggling and selling bootlegged cigarettes, and improving customs and international cooperation (Joossens, 2000). Ultimately, the corrupt cooperation between the tobacco industry, organized crime, and government officials (especially in the developing world) must be rooted out.

3. All countries need to start with basic elements leading to tobacco control, such as frequent national prevalence surveys. (Standardized core questions for such surveys are presented in Table 7.2). This should be followed by gradual but certain steps toward full control, such as advertising bans and restrictions on smoking in public places.

4. Steps need to be taken to develop a supportive environment for tobacco control. Public opinion needs to be mobilized at all levels of society. Smoke-free public areas need to be created or extended (MacKay & Crofton, 1996).

5. Health professionals and officials need to be educated regarding their status as role models and credible sources for smoking prevention.

6. Leaders of various tobacco-control efforts need to integrate their efforts, while other organizations (e.g., youth or women-oriented) need to be encouraged to include tobacco control as part of their agenda.

TABLE 7.2 World Health Organization Global Standardized Guidelines
for Tobacco Use Questions

If only one question can be asked:

1. Do you now smoke daily, occasionally, or not at all?

If two questions can be asked:

1. (same as above) and

2. How many of the following items do you smoke, chew, or apply each day?

    a. manufactured cigarettes

    b. hand-rolled cigarettes

    c. bidis

    d. pipefuls of tobacco

    e. betel quids

    f. snuff

OR

3. Have you ever smoked daily, occasionally, or not at all (or less than 100 cigarettes
in your lifetime)?

If more questions can be asked

1. Have you ever smoked?

2. Have you ever smoked at least 100 cigarettes or the equivalent amount of tobacco
in your lifetime?

3. Have you ever smoked daily?

4. Do you now smoke daily, occasionally, or not at all? On the average, what number
of the following items do/did you smoke per day? (same choices as listed above)

5. How many years have you smoked/did you smoke daily?

6. For ex smokers: How long has it been since you last smoked?

SOURCE: Adapted from MacKay, J., & Crofton, J. (1996).

7. Tobacco companies and industries in each nation need to be investigated
and monitored with respect to their smuggling practices, transnational associations, profits, marketing approaches, and buying of influence. Bans on tobacco
promotion must be considered (MacKay & Crofton, 1996).

8. Balances between nationally and locally initiated efforts, prevention and
cessation programs, and other aspects of an overall tobacco control effort must be
tailored to the realities of each country.

9. Tobacco taxes should be increased. The United States experienced a 4%
decrease in smokers and in cigarettes consumed and a 14% decrease in teen smokers for every 10% increase in tobacco tax (Elder et al., 1996; Lewitt, Coate, &

Grossman, 1981). These gains may be even greater in developing countries (MacKay & Crofton, 1996). Tax revenues may then be earmarked for tobacco-control research (Elder et al., 1996). Legal settlements from antitobacco court cases in the United States or elsewhere should be directed toward domestic control in individual countries as well.

FURTHER READING

The reader is encouraged to review the journal, *Tobacco Control.*

Notes

1. In contrast to proceedings established in The Hague to try Serbian, Central African, and other indicted war criminals, or to the extradition of cocaine lords to the United States, no tobacco industry officials or their well-situated allies have ever faced an international tribunal for the economic, environmental, and public health devastation wreaked by the proliferation of tobacco cultivation and use. Nor has it even been suggested that they be extradited to Colombia or elsewhere to answer for the addictions and deaths they are helping cause abroad.

2. That policy interventions have been successful in controlling the lethal nature of legal substances has never been more clearly demonstrated than in the newly independent states of the former Soviet Union. These states evidenced a decline in alcohol-related chronic disease deaths as well as mortality due to motor vehicle accidents, suicides, and homicides between 1986 and 1988. This good fortune was due to an anti-alcohol campaign launched in 1985 and the restriction of alcohol sales to a small number of legal shops. In 1991, with the dissolution of the Soviet Union and subsequent liberalization of laws, alcohol consumption abruptly increased, as did deaths due to coronary heart disease (Morabia, 2000).

8

Taking on the Wheel of Disease

Health Behavior Change in the 21st Century

Are we winning or losing? Without a doubt, considerable success has been realized in vaccine-preventable diseases, most notably with the eradication of smallpox and the near-elimination of polio. Oral rehydration, where systematically and universally applied, has done much to reduce mortality due to diarrhea. Whether a precursor to or product of the social advancement of women, family-planning efforts have reduced wasteful fertility and improved local and national economies. A spottier track record exists relative to the promotion of adequate nutrition and vector control. Nevertheless, innovations in health communications, contingency management, and community self-control have shown much promise. The suffering caused by the AIDS epidemic continues to accelerate, although certain small successes have been realized. The sinister yet resourceful attack by the tobacco industry on the health and environment of the developing world far outpaces our still modest countermeasures. Nevertheless, recent anti-industry success via media advocacy and legal challenges in the United States, Canada, Australia, and elsewhere provides a blueprint that eventually could be applied universally.

As a comparative summary of the previous chapters, Figure 8.1 represents a report card on progress to date in the various health areas addressed herein, by general categories of interventions. Upstream interventions represented by broad-based policy or social change are characterized on the left of the figure, followed by primary and secondary prevention, and finally containment of outbreaks of illness once they occur. By their nature, vector-borne illnesses, vaccine-preventable diseases, family planning, and HIV/AIDS have been targeted by primary prevention efforts, for the most part, whereas respiratory infections and diarrhea are the subjects of immediate intervention once the illness occurs. To some extent, respiratory infections (through limiting others' exposure) and HIV (through the control of vertical transmission) can be contained, once an individual is infected. Perhaps the most disappointing aspect of this progress report is that tobacco control alone has emphasized media advocacy, policy changes, legal actions, and other broad-based "pre-primary prevention" efforts. And in the case of tobacco control, such emphasis has been witnessed only in industrialized countries and only after years of smoking cessation and similar efforts that chase primarily the "tail end of causality"[1] (McKinlay & Marceau, 1999). The Healthy Cities initiative (Ashton, 1992), which truly examines the entire spectrum of causality, has to date been primarily a northern European and Canadian phenomenon. Therefore, opportunities exist in virtually all areas to improve applications to the entire spectrum of public health interventions for societal and behavioral change.

In short, one might be modestly optimistic about the continued success of health communications, learning theory applications, media advocacy, and community self-control for effective public health behavior change. Such progress would especially hold true if the demographic transition in developing countries imitated that in Europe and in North America in the 19th and early 20th century: Drops in mortality rates and then birth rates would gradually lead to a healthier population at a higher but stable level (Figure 8.2). However, King's (1991) dark prognosis (Chapter 1) portends nearly insurmountable challenges unless intensive and broad-based efforts are undertaken immediately. Initial drops in mortality without checking the birth rate could result in uncontrolled population growth and corresponding habitat destruction, eventually presaging even higher mortality rates (Figure 8.3).

McKinlay and Marceau (2000) agree that the field of public health is at a crossroads and ask: "Should we simply continue traveling on the traditional road . . . or adopt different approaches to reach newly agreed-upon objectives? Public health workers, motivated by humanism and utilitarianism, deserve to get somewhere by design, not just perseverance" (p. 32). Whether it is our health or habitat, our well-being and that of the planet continue to be threatened by consumption of

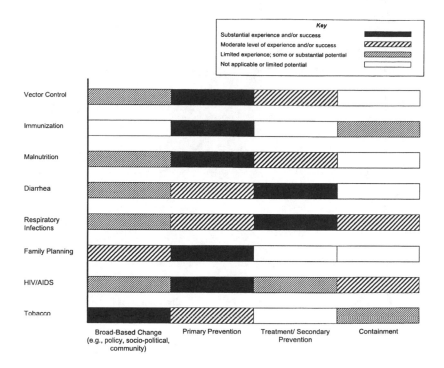

Figure 8.1. A public health report card.

natural resources, population, and inequality. Environmental problems, chronic and infectious diseases, and even social strife appear on the surface to be fairly independent phenomena. Nevertheless, these seemingly disparate factors share certain causal characteristics. To some degree, all are products of inequality among people, are related to population pressures, and, at least to some extent, are associated with human consumption patterns.

Figure 8.4 presents the individual contributions of and interactions among the components of the Wheel of Disease, components that particularly affect health: consumption, population, and inequality. Realizing progress toward the broad goals of the Jakarta Declaration (Chapter 1) requires much more in the way of successful experiences in public health behavior change for family planning, infectious disease control, and the prevention of HIV transmission and nutritional health. An expansion to new targets addressing broader aspects of the Wheel of Disease is needed. These nontraditional roads form the subject of the present chapter.

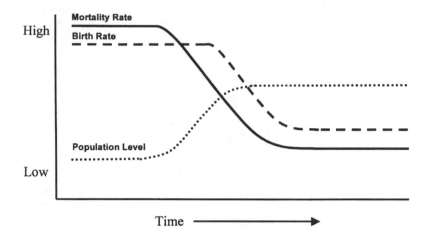

Figure 8.2. Demographic transition model in Western countries.

▦ Consumption

Consumption may be defined as human activity involving the transformation of energy and materials. Although consumption is a natural activity of all creatures, this transformation may be harmful in an economic sense in that such commodities will be less available to future generations and that their use, in turn, may harm or threaten the environment and human health (Myers, 1997). An even more fundamental argument against excessive consumption relates to our obligation as stewards of nature. As Mark Sagoff (1997) writes,

> We take our bearings from the natural world—our sense of time from its days and seasons, our sense of place from the character of a landscape and particular plants and animals native to it. An intimacy with nature ends our isolation in the world. We know where we belong, and we can find the way home. (p. 96)

Nevertheless, humans have always acted consistently with the scriptural injunction to "take dominion" over nature, and they have exploited the environment in the belief that it was so vast and durable that no basic harm could come to it.

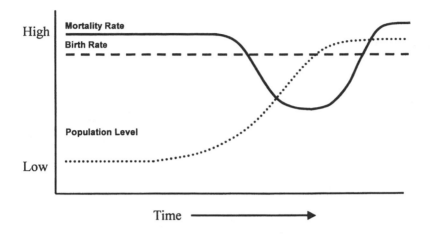

Figure 8.3. Demographic transition model under conditions of unchecked birth rates and environmental collapse.

The wealthy societies of the world consume a vastly disproportionate amount of energy and materials and produce an inordinate amount of waste. For example, in 1996, the United States produced 120% of the carbon emissions that China produced, with 20% of China's population (Myers, 1997), whereas the average American consumed 227 times as much gasoline as the average Indian. One half billion people have an inadequate supply of water today, a number that could rise to 3 billion by the year 2025.

Energy

Increased consumption of natural resources threatens the worldwide environment and has even made parts of the planet virtually uninhabitable. Resources that do exist are not shared equally within or between populations, and the disparity between haves and have-nots is increasing. After World War II, the dominant American economy turned its attention to the comfort and convenience of its consumers, whose demands were met largely by its ever-expanding automobile and other consumer-oriented industries. This trend has converted the United States into the greatest energy-consuming nation in the world. In turn, our energy con-

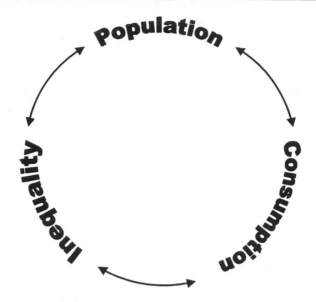

Figure 8.4. The Wheel of Disease.

sumption has resulted in increased exploration for fossil fuels, as well as accelerated ecological harm in wildernesses and other fragile environments through exploration, pumping, or shipping. Polluted air, acid rain, and the greenhouse effect
are all side effects of our excessive consumption. A potentially dangerous technological fix, nuclear energy has been touted as a remedy for our insatiable addiction
to new energy, whereas geothermal, solar, and other renewable resource technologies are far from being adequately developed. Meanwhile, we remain dependent
on foreign oil, in spite of 25 years of federal initiatives to promote self-reliance.
Our addiction stems largely from personal automobiles, accounting for 40% of
energy use compared to less than 1% for buses and 2.2% for rail (Myers, 1992).
Although our fuel efficiency per vehicle has improved, these gains have been ne-
gated by an increase in average distance traveled. In all, our oil dependency has
various unwanted side effects, including an unfavorable balance of trade and national security problems. Oil dependence, for example, was largely responsible
for the 1991 Persian Gulf War.

Boyden and Dovers (1992) have divided human history into four ecological
phases. In the first, the hunter-gatherer phase, the routine use of fire was associated with a doubling of energy use per person, with half of this representing so-
matic energy and the other half extrasomatic energy (e.g., from fire fuels). The

early farming phase was characterized by higher levels of calorie consumption and more stable food supplies. About 200 generations ago, human culture evolved into the early urban phase, as cities began to appear. With this urbanization came social stratification, the military institution, and the advent of infectious diseases as a major cause of mortality. The development of cities also brought the use of timber, fiber, and other natural materials for purposes other than fuel and clothing. Finally, about eight generations ago, humans made the transition to the high-energy-consumption phase. In this phase, calorie consumption in industrializing countries increased to 132% of need, nearly half of the world's drylands became deserts, and worldwide population growth reached 1.6% annually. Although this high-energy-consumption phase is more characteristic of the industrialized world—just as high rates of population growth are more typical in underdeveloped countries—the environmental impact of this consumption is not necessarily suffered by those who consume most. Timber, coffee, meat, seafood, rubber, minerals, and even illegal drugs consumed by the West are often produced at extraordinary cost to the environments of the South, although the economic benefits of their exports accrue to few. Nor is consumption-related pollution limited to the habitats of the industrialized world. Although excess carbon monoxide produced by traffic jams may be localized and pollution in the form of acid rain and fouled river water is shared regionally, global warming and excess ultraviolet radiation may affect people who have made few contributions to the problem (Boyden & Dovers, 1992, p. 64).

Food

Hunger is perhaps the most urgent, compelling, and emotionally charged issue we confront. Excessive consumption of food by a small segment of the world's population exacerbates the perception of inequality and further threatens the environment. Food distribution and consumption issues get much play in the popular media, which has led to certain misconceptions about hunger, including these:

There is not enough food. Two hundred years ago, British economist Thomas Malthus issued his dire prophecy that any further increases in world population, then at 15% of today's level, would lead to massive famine and starvation. Yet even though the globe's population is expanding dramatically, for the present time there remains an abundance of food. By the mid 1990s, world per capita daily calorie supply was 2,740, up 400 calories in 30 years (Reid, 1998). The world already produces enough food to feed perhaps as many as 10 billion vegetarians (Sagoff, 1997), and even most poor countries produce enough food for their people. Although we are getting to the point where there will be too many mouths to feed, human institutions, policies, and economic forces determine who starves and who eats—or allowed to overeat.

Natural disasters are a root cause of hunger. Man-made forces are making increasing numbers of people vulnerable to nature's vagaries. Droughts, the making of deserts, and floods are largely or totally caused by human behavioral patterns. Thus, natural disasters would be better labeled "nature's reactions."

It is a matter of food versus environmental concerns. Environmental damage undercuts our food-producing resources and threatens our health. Each year about 30 million acres of forests are destroyed to make way for agriculture—similar to the rate at which agricultural land is becoming useless through loss of topsoil and desertification. But efforts to feed the hungry are only a small part of the crisis. The production of high-protein foods such as beef not only wastes land, water, and energy but also promotes the destruction of vital rain forests and contributes to erosion and the greenhouse effect. The less we emphasize grains or more efficient meat sources as our source of protein, the more we create environmental damage and contribute to nutritional inequalities.[2] Moreover, atherosclerosis, cancer, and other chronic diseases are directly related to the consumption of high-fat foods, largely from the same sources as those that are inefficient protein sources. Hunting and gathering approaches to fishing have pushed many species to the brink of extinction, whereas aquaculture could meet 40% of consumer demand for this healthy source of animal protein. Crops indigenous to a region, such as wheat in temperate zones and sugar and fruit in the tropics, are more likely to be environmentally friendly within their native latitudes than species transplanted from different climates (Sagoff, 1997).

Healthy diets require substantial amounts of protein and that the best source for this is animal products. Virtually no one who gets an adequate amount to eat will not also get enough protein (Lappe, 1982). Protein-requirement estimates range from 2.5% to 8% of calories, far less than most Americans get—and less than the National Dairy Council and other protein-lobby representatives recommend (Robbins, 1987, p. 172). Moreover, legumes, grains, and vegetables can provide excellent sources of dietary protein and are far more habitat-friendly. Of more personal relevance, nonanimal food sources are less likely to contain unwanted pesticide residues, hormone additives, and other additives increasingly central to the production of meat and dairy products.

Medical Care

Overconsumption may actually affect medical care, as witnessed in the disparity between the universality of health care coverage and its costs in the United States, compared to the situation in similar Western democracies. The American medical culture promotes an overabundance of clinical interventions in both regular medicine and surgery. According to one scholar's opinion (Linsk, 1993), 90% or more of medical costs are generated in the United States because a physician has ordered diagnostic tests, medications or other treatments, consultations, hospitalizations, or surgery. Perhaps as few as 15% of these interventions are supported by scientific evidence for them. The medical culture promotes its tools, and the public gradually begins to expect that the technology will be available and that insurance companies will pay for it.

Equality

The fall of the Berlin Wall culminated an extraordinary sequence of events and brought final closure to Lenin's usurpation of the 1917 Russian Revolution and Hitler's 1939 invasion of Poland. Many have attributed this radical turn in world history to the obvious superiority of the American military and capitalist economy, to the fundamental corruption of the Soviet society, or to both. Conservative politicians assert that the bankruptcy of socialism per se, especially as juxtaposed with capitalism, is the root cause explaining why much of Europe and Asia abandoned Marxism. Thus, we have at least implicitly affirmed that economic might makes right and that economic inequality is an unfortunate but necessary by-product of overall social progress.[3] As a corollary, diseases that affect primarily poorer subgroups or nations are less likely to attract the political attention needed to maintain control efforts (Lederberg, Shope, & Oaks, 1992).

Although the profit motive does, indeed, seem key to economic productivity and growth, equality and health—at least as broadly defined—are critical to ensuring long-term growth, as well. In an economic sense, capital comprises both physical and human aspects. Physical capital—raw materials, roads, commercial vehicles, factories, ports, and the like—are arguably less central to a nation's economic well-being than human capital. The latter, comprising education, experience, and health, is predicated on equality within a society (Barro, 1996).

In an econometric study of 97 nations, Barro (1996) examined the relative contributions to gross domestic product of a variety of factors endogenous and exogenous to each nation. Education, life expectancy at birth, fertility rate, government consumption (nonproductive spending and taxation), adherence to rule-of-law, democracy (access to and participation in the nation's political life), inflation, and investment may all contribute at least partially to economic growth. Health and growth are seen as reciprocally causal: A healthier population produces more, whereas economic advancement may raise the life expectancy of the population.

High fertility rates are strongly related to excessive mortality, which, in turn, slows productivity. Universal education of both genders can be expected to reduce wasteful fertility and improve the economic life of a society.

The overall poverty or wealth of a nation holds limited explanatory power in determining its health. Among pairs of nations with roughly equivalent per capita incomes, Malawi has a fertility rate more than twice as high as Vietnam, the Ivory Coast has an infant mortality rate 30 times greater than Sri Lanka, and Brazil has a mortality rate for children under 5 years old that is twice that of Venezuela (World Bank, 1997, p. 3). Broad access to preventive and curative health care, clean water and sanitation, education, culture, and income distribution accounts for most of these differences. Although global income has increased by 700% since World War II, the rich have been the primary beneficiaries: The wealthiest 20% have increased their share of the world's income from 70% to 85% since 1960, whereas income of the poorest 20% has dropped from 2.3% to 1.4% over this same period (Sagoff, 1997).

Although a frequent critic of the human rights record in China and other countries, the United States—the wealthiest society in history—is itself often put on the defensive for its own record on poverty. Nearly one fifth of households with children fall below the poverty line, and more than 20% of children have no health coverage. Among families headed by single mothers, 39% of whites and 57% of African Americans and Latinos live in poverty. Incredibly, 18% of these latter two groups still fall below the poverty line when the women who head the household have full-time employment (Kosters, 1994).

Equal Opportunity Infections

Malnutrition, limited access to health services, and ignorance, all fellow travelers of poverty and institutionalized prejudice, in turn presage the potential for disease outbreaks. Although Surgeon General David Satcher (1995) advised us that "the health of the individual is best ensured by maintaining or improving the health of the entire community" (p. 2), American national priorities have continued to emphasize diseases of affluence (e.g., both obesity and anorexia nervosa). Infectious diseases tend to get little attention until they pose a threat to affluent populations (Farmer, 1996). For example, tuberculosis has not been a leading cause of death among adults in the industrialized world since early in the 1900s, but it has not really lost any ground worldwide. Its label as a "reemerging" disease is more the sounding of an alarm that it is emerging from the ranks of the poor. Immigration and close quartering of the poor in shelters, slums, and prisons have accelerated the spread of tuberculosis in the United States.

HIV transmission clearly could threaten anyone but, statistically speaking, does not do so equally. HIV maintains its potency among the poor and marginalized people of society. Transmission of HIV to women now occurs at the rate of 3,000 per day. The second-class social status and economic dependence of women, as well as the cultural double standard reflected in norms governing sexual behavior, are largely responsible for this unchecked increase (Aral, 1993).

Even chronic diseases strike the poor more than the middle and upper classes. Americans 45 to 64 years of age with annual incomes less than $10,000, compared to their age counterparts with incomes at $35,000 or above, have a 1.6 relative risk of heart disease, a 1.4 relative risk of hypertension, a 6.9 relative risk of emphysema, and a 1.3 relative risk of chronic bronchitis (Watanabe, 1997). Thus, the poor experience the diseases of affluence without its pleasures.

Population

Recent progress in population control in Asia, Mexico, and elsewhere have led some to opine that there is virtually nothing to worry about. Referring to the decline in fertility in Europe and elsewhere in recent years, Singer (1999) asserts that "people's personal decisions about how many children they want can make the world population go anywhere—to zero or 100 billion or more" (p. 25). Does Singer have this right? In regions where population growth remains out of control, "people's personal decisions" are largely dictated by extreme poverty and a lack of education. Moreover, the women who bear the bulk of the world's new babies seldom get to participate in these personal decisions. Although I would certainly like to share Singer's optimism, I fear we cannot sit back and observe continued population growth; conversely, a reduction in population would certainly create new social stresses but could perhaps prove beneficial to all species, humans included.

Population interacts substantially with the Wheel of Disease's other two components as well. As indicated in Figure 8.5, family planning is less likely to take root in societies where women have lower status and less control over their reproductive health. In addition, some parents will continue to have children until one or more male offspring are born, a particular threat to China's One Child Policy. Among other factors, male children are seen as better able to provide the parents a comfortable retirement. Children in this and other ways are viewed as a kind of consumer good, with *more* being equivalent to *better.*

The Interaction Between Inequality and Consumption

In an eloquent essay on the relationship between equality and consumption, Obiora (1999) described local and international issues related to environmental justice. Environmental injustice, in its most extreme form, was manifested in the execution of Ken Saro-Wiwa and several of his fellow Ogoni tribesmen by the Nigerian government nearly a decade ago. The Ogonis strongly objected to the destruction of the environment in their region of Nigeria by Shell Oil Company and its aggressive oil drilling and production activities. Saro-Wiwa was effective in garnering international attention and sympathy for his efforts, thereby offending the tyrannical military regime in Lagos. As Shell Oil looked the other way, the military regime put Saro-Wiwa and several of his colleagues on trial and, through a kangaroo court process, found them guilty of treason and had them executed. Although the international community was justifiably outraged by this action, Obiora pointed out that the very same community's implicit insatiable appetite for petroleum and explicit tolerance of Shell Oil's activities in Nigeria were probably responsible for the conflict between the Ogonis and the military junta in the first place.

Obiora (1999) described how the predatory practices of political and economic elites, juxtaposed with minimal options for impoverished minorities and less developed countries, trigger a cycle of economic and environmental degradation. Growth-oriented principles so popular in the post-Cold War era benefit primarily those who have the capital to participate in the world economy in the first place. Both the benefits of environmental exploitation and the costs or burdens of that exploitation are unevenly distributed, with poor individuals in wealthy countries and less developed countries drawing the short straw each time. Approaches to environmental reform involve "command and control regulation," market-based incentives, and redress through criminal and tort law. However, these

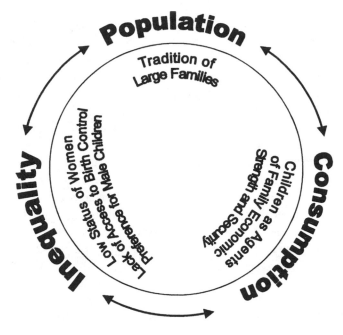

Figure 8.5. The Wheel of Disease applied to family planning.

legal and political solutions often highlight the tension between human rights and environmental protection.

Nor are the world's large stock exchanges solely responsible for the disadvantages suffered by people of poor nations. The tendency of generally liberal environmental organizations to "give primacy to penguins and parks over local populations" may actually exacerbate the problems of environmental injustice (Obiora, 1999, p. 475). Poor communities tend to see the approaches of these organizations as luxuries they cannot afford. The human factor cannot be discounted in ecological programs. Sustainable development embraces both environmentalism and economic development. It refers to the promotion of human well-being without the decline of natural resources and biological development (Anaya & Crider, 1996).

Environmental justice requires a grassroots approach to sustainable development, concurrently addressing both social and environmental concerns. Environmental justice efforts should distribute environmental amenities more equitably, redress environmental abuses, and distribute the burden of environmental protection. Thus, environmental justice seeks to reverse the decades-long trend in the

United States and other northern countries of situating polluting industries in neighborhoods inhabited by people of color and poverty. This path of less resistance steers such industries away from middle-class NIMBY (not in my backyard) activists and toward neighborhoods with minimal political participation or clout. Cheap land values in such neighborhoods attract both polluting industries and impoverished residents (Obiora, 1999, p. 481).

A new paradigm is required if progress is to be achieved in the area of environmental justice. Societies must be convinced to live off of nature's income, rather than squandering its capital. In other words, the abundance produced by natural resources can contribute to the economic betterment of human society, but exploiting nonrenewable resources must be undertaken conservatively. Nations and regions must be held responsible for protecting the flora and fauna in their territory. The worldwide trend toward more democratic governance should bode well for environmental reform and protection, as well, if equity issues are addressed both within and between nations.

The Interaction Between Population and Consumption

In his essay, "Nature's Limits," Lester Brown (1995) discussed the optimistic outcome of the 1994 international conference on population and development in Cairo. The general theme of that conference was emphasis on the need to stabilize human numbers at a maximum of 8 billion or 9 billion. Such maintenance would contribute to an environmentally sustainable society. However, to accomplish this, women worldwide would have to be able to manage and control their own fertility and their own lives. For this and other reasons, the Cairo goals seem quite ambitious. Nevertheless, if humans fail to act quickly to control the population, the food shortages that this population is contributing to will do it for us. The Earth has natural limitations, in spite of extraordinary growth in food productivity in the last half of the 20th century. Brown noted that something will have to give soon when it comes to the Earth's resources. Three specific limits on food production are already occurring: the decline in both oceanic and fresh-water fisheries, the amount of fresh water produced by the hydrological cycle, and the amount of fertilizer that existing crop varieties can effectively use. The world fish catch, for instance, now fourfold that of 1960, is no longer rising and apparently is actually beginning to diminish. Concern over water scarcity and the degradation of fresh-water reservoirs worldwide brings into question whether we can even slake the thirst of the world's population, let alone feed it.

The world's birds may literally be serving as canaries in the coal mine. About two thirds of the 9,600 species are in decline. Deforestation, wetland drainage and destruction, air and water pollution, acid rain, and hunting all have contributed to this appalling figure.

The depletion of society's natural capital—namely forests, range lands, top-soil, fresh-water aquifers, and fish stocks, as well as air and water pollution, has begun to affect regional economies through loss of jobs and of exports. For example, forest destruction in various tropical countries has led to industry collapse and related job and income loss and export reductions. Use of underground-aquifer water resources now exceeds the recharging of these aquifers and will eventually result in the reduction of available farmland for agriculture. The world's food staple, rice, is especially affected by aquifer depletion, as it requires an extraordinary amount of irrigation. According to Brown (1995),

Fish trapping such as that shown here in a Nepalese river has for millennia helped meet basic nutrition needs for communities throughout the world. The sustainability of this consumption, however, is now severely threatened by increased population pressure and the catching of smaller and smaller fish, water pollution, and the reduction of water available through the hydrological cycle.

> The ecological symptoms of unsustainability include shrinking forests, thinning soils, depleted aquifers, collapsing fisheries, expanding deserts, and rising global temperatures. The economic symptoms include economic decline, fallen incomes, rising unemployment, price instability, and a loss of investor confidence. The political and social symptoms include hunger and malnutrition, and, in extreme cases, mass starvation; environmental and economic refugees; social conflicts along ethnic, tribal, and religious lines; and riots and insurgencies. (p. 14)

Unfortunately, once demands rise beyond sustainable yields, future growth is maintained only by consuming the forest, fishery, or other resource base itself. These thresholds may be crossed directly or indirectly: For example, deforestation and a range-land degradation through excessive demands for forest and livestock products will increase the amount of rainfall runoff, reducing the amount retained and absorbed for aquifer recharge. Governments often actually encourage unsustainable consumption. For example, much of Amazon basin agricultural production relies wholly on governmental tax support for profitability. Investors and consumers alike must come to grips with the fact that the consumption of rain forest beef is more or less equivalent to the consumption of the rain forest itself. Thus, the "hamburger debate"—equating the proliferation of fast-food hamburger-oriented restaurants, steak, and other beef dishes to habitat harm—will eventually take center stage in forcing consumers from wealthy countries to recognize the impact they have on the global environment (Browder, 1988).

A test case for crossing the threshold of consumption of sustainable and renewable resources will take place in China. Given its unique combination of population growth, starting from a base of the world's largest population, and its unprecedented economic growth, China will rapidly develop into a society no longer able to meet its own food-related needs. By the year 2030, China's annual demand for grain alone will increase to 479 million tons, forcing it to import 216 million tons. In 1993, all of the nations of the world exported only 200 million tons, and this figure does not consider that China's population will continue to express a preference for more meat, eggs, beer, and other inefficient consumer products (Brown, 1995). During this same period of time, the United States, with its long-running grain surpluses, will add another 100 million or so individuals, eventually reaching the point where none of its grain will be available for export. Clearly, the potential for worldwide disruption is substantial, given China's increasing political, economic, and military power.

▨ The Interaction Among All Wheel Components

Figure 8.4 represents the interactive nature of population, consumption, and inequality and implies the need to consider all three factors, regardless of a specific intervention emphasis. In other words, directly addressing population issues (e.g., through family planning programs; see Chapter 4) without considering inequality and (to a lesser extent) consumption will eventually prove inadequate, regardless of any short-term gains that may be realized. For example, ever-increasing demand for goods and services requires more people to produce them, leading to pressure to increase the population through birth or immigration.

Most public health programs, however, address targets not specifically in these three categories. How then are they relevant to intervention issues in general? Let's consider the topic of transportation safety and related problems (see Figure 8.6. Clearly, the presence of more people on the road (population) increases the probability of motor vehicle accidents; different insurance rates for urban versus rural drivers bear testimony to this. Consumption is a clear culprit, pressuring policy makers to maximize speed limits, minimize fuel prices, and relax fleet fuel-efficiency standards, maintaining the automobile's primacy as a form of personal transportation.

Where does inequality fit in? Poorer people are faced with three choices: (a) drive older, less reliable cars that are (presumably) less dependable and more polluting; (b) buy smaller autos that do not stand up as well in crashes; and/or (c) choose inconvenient public transportation, which in worst-case scenarios may also be unsafe due to the potential for crime.

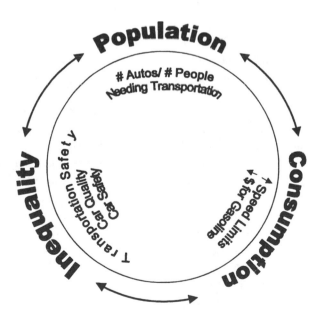

Figure 8.6. The Wheel of Disease applied to transportation-related accidents.

Many chronic and infectious diseases have primary roots in just two of the Wheel's three elements. For instance, tuberculosis stems largely from poverty (inadequate nutrition, poor housing) and to some extent from overcrowding. Causal factors related to cancer and heart disease have obvious ties with excessive consumption (of high-fat foods and tobacco) and poverty (e.g., lack of access to screening and early treatment; unsafe or inadequate physical activity access). However, even certain diseases in these two categories share all three causal factors. For instance, dengue fever, spread by the *Aedes aegypti* mosquito (see Chapter 5), strikes primarily in heavily urbanized areas (population); requires standing water for reproducing, including that found in carelessly discarded garbage (consumption); and is more likely to strike where households have neither the time nor resources for adequate cleaning or insecticide purchase (inequality) (Gubler, 1989).

The Crux of the Argument: "Risk Factorology" Versus "Public Health Nihilism"

Given the overwhelming challenge presented by the three components of the Wheel, the reader may despair of the utility of investing the energy required to make a significant public health impact, especially in areas of child survival, family planning, and the environment. Although a major theme of this book centers on the search for broad social, demographic, and ecological causality and parallel upstream interventions, small-scale and focused public health research and programming will continue to play an important role, not only in relatively conservative public health systems such as that in the United States but also in countries that maintain a social welfare emphasis within public health.

Fairchild and Oppenheimer's (1998) review of the history of progress in tuberculosis control over the past 150 years reinforces this point. They began by exploring the work of physician-historian Thomas McKeown, who examined reasons for the decline in mortality in Britain (McKeown, Record, & Turner, 1975). Among the factors studied were clinical and public health initiatives (especially the segregation of infected individuals) and broader social changes, such as improved educational standards, better housing, and improved nutritional status of the population. Of these and other factors, McKeown determined that nutritional gains were responsible for the bulk of the reduction in tuberculosis rates, implying that although well-intentioned, public health measures were largely misguided and wasteful. He would, thus, agree with McKinlay and Marceau's (2000) criticism that much of epidemiology (and by its extension, public health) is based on "risk factorology:" a never-ending, circular, and ultimately fruitless quest for the set of biological and behavioral risk factors that are associated with a disease, without addressing the true socioeconomic roots of the problem.

Although McKeown's thesis has been given credit for a more progressive "New Public Health" (Ashton, 1992), Fairchild and Oppenheimer (1998) are concerned that its logical extension would lead us to a "public health nihilism,"[4] and they take issue both with some of the specifics of the tuberculosis example and the more general notion that public health can advance without specifically targeted interventions. They note that sanitariums played a major role in controlling the spread of tuberculosis, at least in Germany, the United States, and other industrialized nations. The combined forces of veterinary science and public health eradicated bovine tuberculosis, a special threat to children into the early part of the 20th century. Nor have disease- and risk factor-oriented interventions been without success. The census-based, impact-oriented (CBIO) approach to primary health care in Bolivia appears not only to alleviate the suffering of those at highest risk in communities but at the same time to be highly acceptable to community stakeholders (Perry et al., 1999).

Sagoff (1997) argues that technological advances in energy, agriculture, forestry, and manufacturing will allow the planet to experience continued economic growth concurrent with improvements in the quality of life. Progress in current public health challenges (e.g., AIDS, vector-borne disease control) will surely continue to demand advances both in the overall welfare of the population and in specific clinical and public health technology—including the technology of promoting behavior change. Indeed, attention to a behavior-change emphasis, particularly if it involves the behavior of policy makers as well as the population, will diminish frustration and pessimism that often accompany efforts to brake the Wheel of Disease.

New Targets for Behavior Change

Agrodiversity

Ecological issues such as biodiversity and environmentally friendly agriculture have received insufficient attention from behavior-change experts. A possible horizon opening up in this arena is agrodiversity. Brookfield and Padoch (1994) define crop biodiversity as the number and diversity of species used by farmers in their cultivation activities and the number of wild or semidomesticated species used for food and other economic products. They point out that such biodiversity is rapidly diminishing, as we rely increasingly on fewer and fewer highly cultivated species for our foodstuffs. However, small farmers have typically been blamed for much of the reduction in crop biodiversity and degradation of land, when in truth, traditional approaches to biodiversity are probably consistent with a wider framework called agrodiversity.

Agrodiversity comprises the ways in which farmers use the natural diversity of the environment for production of their crops as well as management of land and water as a whole. For example, slash-and-burn agricultural activity may not necessarily be bad if not done on a wholesale level. Many slash-and-burn farmers extend their activity only a short distance into a forest, plant their crops for one or two seasons, and allow the forest to reclaim and regenerate the land. Large-scale farmers are far more likely to destroy large areas of forests and other land with their less sensitive cultivation procedures.

The creeping effects of land shortage, however, in response to both population and commercial pressures, may result in the reduction or elimination of the fallow periods necessary for regenerating the land. Brookfield and Padoch (1994) point out that "listening to the small farmer" may be the best approach to studying sustainable agriculture in meeting the needs of increased population. According to them,

> A study of farmers' knowledge[5] is essential as is an understanding of how the knowledge is both developed and transferred. Clearly the role of extension officers is only one part of the whole story. It is essential to move away from the discredited image of the . . . scientist with all the answers; to find out how resources are really used and why; to learn what specific problems most need to be researched; and to determine what existing research and resource management has real value. Collaboration between farmers and by farmers with scientists . . . is essential if the accelerating growth of problems is to be met with an equal set of responses. (p. 41)

Both behavioral science research and health-psychology intervention expertise would greatly contribute to confronting these and related problems.

Sustainable Consumption

Changing consumption-related activities. Young and Sachs (1995) talk about the challenges facing us in attempting to create a sustainable "materials economy." Faced with a passion for consumption, societies will soon run out of raw materials needed to satisfy this hunger and will start consuming the base. Young and Sachs define five different consumption-related activities contributing to this threat and discuss opportunities for making major improvements in these activities. Their positions are summarized in Table 8.1. Clearly, using Young and Sachs's opportunities to promote sustainable consumption will entail imaginative combinations of communications and marketing, contingency management, media advocacy, and community self-control.

Socially responsible purchasing. Published by the Council on Economic Priorities (1989), *Shopping for a Better World* takes a step beyond sustainable consumption to focus on the consumer society as a potential major catalyst for social change. This pocket-size guide directs shoppers toward the products of companies that are relatively socially responsible. The dimensions that are rated include donations to charity, promotion of women's and minority advancement, military contracts, use of animal testing, the disclosure of information, the amount of community outreach, association with nuclear power, environmental friendliness including the promotion of recycling, and other topics that may vary in timeliness from year to year. For example, to achieve the top rating in charitable donations, 2% or more of the net pretax earnings of the corporation must be given to charity. Between 1% and 2% results in the second level of rating, 0.6% to 1% the third level, and 0.6% or less the lowest level. In terms of women's advancement, having at least two women on the board of directors and one at a vice presidential level or higher yields a top rating, whereas having one woman on the board or one at the vice presidential level the second rating. The same criteria are applied to minority advancement. Companies that conduct no animal testing rate the top level, whereas companies that have reduced the number of animals used in testing and have developed alternative research methods achieve the second level.

Shopping for a Better World also comments on the process of conducting the ratings. In terms of disclosure of information, companies sending back completed questionnaires rate the top level, whereas partially completed questionnaires with important information unanswered rate the middle level. Companies sending only annual reports or proxy statements rate the lowest level. Companies with strong programs promoting health education, housing, and volunteerism rated the top level of community outreach, whereas companies that promote recycling, alternative energy sources, and waste reduction, having no major regulatory violations, get the top level for environmental friendliness.

The Council rated hundreds of common consumer products on these criteria. For instance, someone buying Wheaties will be buying from a corporation with a solid record on women and minority advancement as well as community out-

TABLE 8.1 Consumer-Related Activities That Threaten the Environment and Opportunities for Change

Activity	Example	Opportunity
Mining and drilling	The mining of relatively high-grade ore until this ore is extracted and the mining enterprise moves on to a new site, rather than continuing to extract low-grade ore, as land is artificially cheap in both the old and new site.	The mining of relatively high grade ore until this ore is extracted and the mining enterprise moves on to a new site, rather than continuing to extract low-grade ore, as land is artificially cheap in both the old and new site.
Manufacturing	Most paper products (especially office paper and boxing) can be made with less than half virgin wood fiber with no loss of quality. Community recycling programs have to be in place to provide a consistent supply of recycled paper.	Making paper from high-percentage virgin wood fiber.
Product design	The design of cheap products that compete at lower retail prices but do not last very long.	Design should emphasize durability and repairability, which ultimately would be less costly to the consumer and at the same time reduce materials consumption.
City planning	Planned communities (or unplanned) in which residences are far from workplaces and services.	Planning needs to be developed that puts people closer to what they need and where they work and that makes more efficient use of already developed land, thereby reducing the need for materials-intensive construction and disruption of land previously dedicated to agriculture or in its natural state.
Direct consumption	Society stresses immediate convenience of consumption and disposal as being "good" without considering issues related to sustainable consumption.	Making changes in consumption patterns to promote a culture of conservation will save both money and materials. Examples are bringing one's own basket to the supermarket, using public transportation, and photo-copying on both sides of a page.

SOURCE: Adapted from Young & Sachs, 1995.

reach, and no animal testing in its portfolio. Mixed records are presented for donations to charity and for disclosure and environmental concerns. Grapenuts also is owned by a company with solid women and minority advancement records and no animal testing. However, its parent company rates poorly on giving to charity and environmental concerns, and it has a mixed record on disclosure and community outreach. Also, the parent company marketed cigarettes (or at least did so when this brochure was published).

Shopping for a Better World seeks to educate consumers about more socially responsible shopping, with an emphasis similar to *What in the World. . . . Shopping*'s primary purpose, however, is to use this leverage to promote more responsible corporate policies among companies from which consumers purchase goods. Presumably, concern about market loss would lead corporations to promote women and minorities, limit animal testing, and divest tobacco products. This media advocacy approach offers substantially more opportunity for creating truly healthier environments than approaches that change one person at a time.

Why, then, do we not see more media advocacy in health behavior-change efforts? Funding for health programs tends to occur on a governmental basis (or in the case of bilateral or multilateral foreign aid, government to government). Most governments, those in developing countries certainly being no exceptions, are paternalistic and conservative in nature. Thus, they may have little inclination to allow the promotion of community self-control, let alone an aggressive and potentially broader based media advocacy. Fostering women's rights, prioritizing the environment over profit, and reducing inequality are not going to be universally embraced for the foreseeable future. The continued imaginative use of social marketing and contingency management, supplemented by media advocacy and community self-control when possible, will prove our best hope for controlling the ravages of the Wheel of Disease.

Conclusions: New Directions for Public Health Promotion

What can behavior-change experts do to contribute to global change and international public health? How can international health experts take advantage of the methodologies of behavioral science? Many options exist, including the following:

Continue to advance theory development (McKinlay & Marceau, 2000) and employ technologies and interventions such as learning theory, health communications and social marketing, media advocacy, and community empowerment.

Specifically, such interventions will target (a) the availability of protective or harmful consumer products; (b) physical, structural, and environmental factors that make health behavior more or less likely to occur; (c) social structures, such as policies, laws, and their enactment and enforcement; and (d) media and cultural communication (Cohen et al., 2000).

Continue to revise the concept of a healthy community. Much development work has emphasized traditional, rural communities. Yet, the rapid urbanization and industrialization in many poorer countries presents a far more complicated picture than we faced 20 years ago. These countries now face not only public health problems like those affecting the West (air and water pollution, waste disposal, etc.) but also many that the West has already overcome (e.g., water safety, sanitation, population expansion). Community organization efforts can no longer target "Healthy Cities" per se but instead must identify neighborhoods and communities within these cities (Harpham, 1991; Rice & Rasmusson, 1992).

Broaden the scope of practice and inquiry, within the context of current domestic health promotion efforts, to include environmental protection, immunizations, family planning and teen pregnancy, and malnutrition.

Develop changes in academic curricula and training opportunities that would alter the focus of health-related behavioral sciences (such as health psychology) from primarily chronic disease prevention to other domestic opportunities as well as international ones. Credit should be given for practica and internships abroad, such as those occasionally available through U.S., Canadian, and other bilateral assistance agencies; the World Health Organization or its regional offices (WHO, PAHO, etc.), or any of numerous nongovernmental organizations (NGOs) involved in family planning, child survival, AIDS control, or other international health targets. For those wishing to invest the time, the Peace Corps offers invaluable experiences for international health practitioners.

Use classroom training to prepare students for possible public health work. Existing courses (e.g., in tobacco control) should be retooled to ensure international content. Students should be encouraged to pursue proficiency in a foreign language, and they should have the opportunity to do so. Thesis and other research requirements could be met through international practica experiences or by analyzing existing sets of data collected abroad. Opportunities to pursue concurrently the behavioral science PhD and MPH, now available in a few universities, should be expanded.

Weigh international experience heavily in admissions decisions for graduate training. Also, opportunities should be expanded for individuals already working abroad—whether they are beginning a Peace Corps assignment or already seasoned professionals—to begin graduate training while abroad via distance learning mechanisms.

These and other opportunities and changes in the behavioral sciences hold the potential to make a strong imprint on the field of international health in the coming decades. In turn, international health expertise will make the health behavior-change disciplines more robust and relevant. But most important, the continued articulation between the two holds substantial promise for alleviating the global burden of disease, as well as the patterns of inequality, consumption, and population that underlie this burden.

SUMMARY

Behavior-change strategies for public health in developing countries have developed at different paces, depending on the target area. HIV/AIDS and tobacco use threaten to wipe out gains realized in nutrition, family planning, and the control of most infectious diseases. Three factors are common to most health problems, and these are represented as the Wheel of Disease. The individual contributions of and interactions among inequality, population, and consumption will continue to stymie public health efforts. A middle ground between risk factorology and public health nihilism must be found. Health psychology, community health education, and other disciplines that emphasize public health behavior change must devote more effort to these upstream issues while maintaining a firm grounding in theory. Changes in the culture of health behavior training and practice will ensure its relevance for decades to come and hold the promise of improving the public's health in developing and developed countries alike.

Notes

1. For example, recent initiatives from the National Institutes of Health have included research to determine whether genetic propensity to tobacco addiction exists, implying a less than full commitment to focus upstream.

2. It takes about 3 kilograms of grain or soy to produce 1 kilogram of poultry or eggs; 6 kilograms per kilogram of pork, and 16 kilograms per kilogram of beef. A slaughter pig provides a calorie supply sufficient for maintaining human life for 49 days, whereas the grain the pig consumed could sustain life for 500 days (Reid, 1998).

3. As Mullan (2000) noted, this societal trend may be reflected in public health professionalism, as well. Public health practitioners and academics have always included idealists with visions (Don Quixotes), clever bureaucrats and politicians with the cunning and calculation to get things done (Machiavellis), and policy makers who see equity of wealth and resources as an important end in itself (Robin Hoods). But Mullan notes that the latter Robin Hood group has been slowly disappearing from the landscape, due more to sociopolitical forces rather than to a lessening need for resource distribution.

4. Fairchild and Oppenheimer (1998) attribute this phrase to Ronald Bayer, a scholar in the area of AIDS and reproductive freedom.

5. We would add or even place much greater emphasis on practice.

References

Academy for Educational Development. (1995). *A tool box for building health communication capacity.* Washington, DC: Author.

Africa AIDS crisis. (2000, January 13). *International Herald Tribune* [Editorial], p. 8.

Aikens, M., Fox-Rushby, J., D'Alessandro, U., Langerock, P., Cham, K., New, L., Bennett, S., Greenwood, B., & Mills, A. (1998). The Gambian national impregnated bednet programme: Costs, consequences, and net cost-effectiveness. *Social Science and Medicine, 46*(2), 181-191.

Amarillo, M., Lansang, M., Bilizario, V., Miguel, C., & Sepulveda, A. (1999, March 2). *Malarial monitoring boards: Keeping the community informed.* Paper presented at the 16th Congress of the International Clinical Epidemiology Network, Bangkok.

Anaya, S. J., & Crider, S.T. (1996). Indigenous peoples, the environment, and commercial forestry in developing countries: The case of Awa Tingni, Nicaragua. *Human Rights Quarterly, 18*(2), 345-367.

Anderson, R. (1992). Some aspects of sexual behavior and the potential demographic impact of AIDS in developing countries. *Social Science and Medicine, 34*(3), 271-280.

Aplasca, M. R., Siegel, D., Mandel, J. S., Santana-Arciaga, R. T., Paul, J., Hudes, E. S., Monzon, O. T., & Hearst, N. (1995). Results of a model AIDS prevention program for high school students in the Philippines. *AIDS, 9*(Suppl. 1) 7-13.

Aral, S. O. (1993). Heterosexual transmission of HIV: The role of other sexually transmitted infections and behavior in its epidemiology and control. *Annual Review of Public Health, 14,* 451-467.

Ashton, J. (1991). The origins of healthy cities. In J. Ashton (Ed.), *Healthy cities* (pp. 1-12). Buckingham, UK: Open University Press.

Asma, S., & Pederson, L. (1999). Tobacco control in Africa: Opportunities for prevention. *Tobacco Control, 8,* 353-354.

Baer, E. C. (1981). Promoting breastfeeding: A national responsibility. *Studies in Family Planning, 12,* 198.

Baingana, G., Choi, K. H., Barrett, D. C., Byansi, R., & Hearst, N. (1995). Female partners of AIDS patients in Uganda: Reported knowledge, perceptions, and plans. *AIDS* (Suppl. 1), 15-19.

Balabanova, D., Bobak, M., & McKee, M. (1998). Patterns of smoking in Bulgaria. *Tobacco Control, 7,* 383-385.

Bandura, A. (1977a). Self-efficacy: Toward a unifying theory of behavioral change. *Psychological Review, 84*(2), 191-215.

Bandura, A. (1977b). *Social learning theory.* Englewood Cliffs, NJ: Prentice Hall.

Banerji, D. (1999). A fundamental shift in the approach to international health by WHO, UNICEF, and the World Bank: Instances of the practice of "intellectual fascism" and totalitarianism in some Asian countries. *International Journal of Health Services, 29*(2), 227-259.

Barro, R. J. (1996). *Health and economic growth.* Unpublished manuscript, Harvard University.

Barrowclough, J. (1997). A way forward for the promotion of health through breastfeeding. *Midwives, 1110*(1308), 16-19.

Basch, P. (1991). A historical perspective on international health. *Infectious Disease Clinics of North America, 5*(2), 183-196.

Basch, P. (1999). *Textbook of international health* (2nd ed.). New York: Oxford University Press.

Basu, R., & Jezek, Z. (1978). Operation Smallpox Zero. *Indian Journal of Public Health, 22*(1), 38-54.

Batholet, J. (2000, January 17). The plague years. *Newsweek,* pp. 32-37.

Bennett, T. (1999). Preventing trafficking in women and children in Asia: Issues and options. *Impact on HIV, 1*(2), 8-13.

Berelson, B. (1969). Beyond family planning. *Studies in Family Planning, 38,* 17-27.

Bhave, G., Lindman, C. P., Hudes, E. S., Desai, S., Wagle, U., Tripathi, S. P., & Mandel, J. S. (1995). Impact of an intervention on HIV, sexually transmitted diseases, and condom use among sex workers in Bombay, India. *AIDS, 9*(Suppl. 1), 21-30.

Biddulph, J. (1981). Promotion of breastfeeding: Experience in Papua New Guinea. In D. Jelliffe & E. Jelliffe (Eds), *Advances in international maternal and child health* (Vol. 1, pp. 164-169). New York: Oxford University Press.

Black, R. (1999, September 21). *Nutritional aspects of child survival.* Paper presented at the X Escuela de Verano de Salud Pública, Mahón, Spain.

Bloom, P. N., & Novelli, W. D. (1981). Problems and challenges of social marketing. *Journal of Marketing, 45,* 79-88.

Boyden, S., & Dovers, S. (1992). Natural-resource consumption and its environmental impacts in the western world: Impacts of increasing per capita consumption. *Ambio, 21,* 63-68.

Braudel, F. (1984). *Bebidas y excitantes.* Madrid: Editorial Alianza.

Brookfield, H., & Padoch, C. (1994). Appreciating agrodiversity: A look at the dynamism and diversity of indigenous farming practices. *Environment, 36*(5), 7-45.

Browder, J. O. (1988). The social cost of rain forest destruction: A critique in economic analysis of the hamburger debate. *Interciencia, 13*(3), 115-120.

Brown, K., & Solomon, N. (1991). Nutritional problems of developing countries. *Infectious Disease Clinics of North America, Edition on International Health, 5*(2), 297-317.

Brown, L. R. (1995). Nature's limits. In L. Brown, C. Flavin, & H. French (Eds), *State of the world* (pp. 3-20). New York: Norton.

Bunch, R. (1982). *Two ears of corn: A guide to people-centered agricultural improvement.* Oklahoma City, OK: World Neighbors.

Cartoux, M., Sombie, I., Van de Perre, P., Meda, N., Tiendrebeogo, S., & Dabis, F. (1999). Evaluation of 2 techniques of HIV pre-test counseling for pregnant women in West Africa. DITRAME Study Group. *International Journal of STD and AIDS, 10*(3), 199-201.

Celentano, D. D., Nelson, K. E., Lyles, C. M., Beyrer, C., Eiumtrakul, S., Go, V. F., Kuntolbutra, S., & Khamboonruang, C. (1998). Decreasing incidence of HIV and sexually transmitted diseases in young Thai men: Evidence for success of the HIV/AIDS control and prevention program. *AIDS, 12*(5), F29-36.

CHANGE Project. (1999). *Innovative approaches and tools for change.* Washington, DC: Academy for Educational Development.

Chapman, S. (1994). Tobacco and deforestation in the developing world. *Tobacco Control, 3,* 191-193.

Chowdhury, A. M. R. (1999). Success with the DOTS strategy. *Lancet, 353,* 1003-1004.

Chowdhury, A. M. R., Chowdhury, S., Islam, M. N., Islam, A., & Vaughn, J. P. (1997). Control of tuberculosis by community health workers in Bangladesh. *Lancet, 350,* 169-172.

Cleland, J. G., Ali, M. M., & Capo-Chichi, V. (1999). Post-partum sexual abstinence in West Africa: Implications for AIDS-control and family planning programmes. *AIDS, 13*(1), 125-131.

Cohen, D., Scribner, R., & Farley, T. (2000). A structural model of health behavior: A pragmatic approach to explain and influence health behaviors at the population level. *Preventive Medicine, 30,* 146-154.

Cortés, M., & Elder, J. (2000). Políticas públicas saludables. El caso del tabaco. In A. Sarría (Ed.), *Promoción de la salud en la comunidad* (pp. 274-303). Madrid, Spain: Universidad Nacional de Educación a Distancia.

Council on Economic Priorities. (1989). *Shopping for a better world: The quick and easy guide to all your socially responsible shopping.* San Francisco: Sierra Club Books.

Crowley, G. (2000, January 17). Fighting the disease: What can be done. *Newsweek,* p. 38.

Cutts, F. T. (1998). Advances and challenges for the expanded programme on immunization. *British Medical Bulletin, 54*(2), 445-461.

Davey, S. (1997). *Polio: The beginning of the end.* Geneva: World Health Organization.

Divan, V. K., & Thorson, A. (1999). Sex, gender, and tuberculosis. *Lancet, 353,* 1000-1001.

Dowdle, W., & Hopkins, D. (1998). *The eradication of infectious diseases.* New York: John Wiley.

Duhl, L. (1986). Healthy cities: Its function and its future. *Health Promotion 1,* 55-60.

Dye, C., Garnett, G. P., Sleeman, K., & Williams, B. G. (1998). Prospects for worldwide tuberculosis control under the WHO DOTS strategy. *Lancet, 352,* 1886-1891.

Elder, J. P., Ayala, G. X., Zabinski, M., Prochaska, J., & Gehrman, C. (2000). Theories, models, and methods of health promotion in rural settings. In B. E. Quill & Loue (Eds.), *Handbook of rural health.* New York: Plenum.

Elder, J., & Douglass, E. (1996). *Behavior change for promoting better environments: Ideas for a national strategy.* Cebu City, Philippines: Greencom Project.

Elder, J., Edwards, C., Conway, T., Kenney, E., Johnson, C. A., & Bennett, D. E. (1996). Independent evaluation of the California Tobacco Education Program. *Public Health Reports, 111,* 353-358.

Elder, J., & Estey, J. (1992). Behavior change strategies for family planning. *Social Science and Medicine, 35*(8), 1065-1076.

Elder, J. P., Geller, E. S., Hovell, M. F., & Mayer, J. A. (1994). *Motivating health behavior.* Albany, NY: Delmar.

Elder, J., Louis, T., Sutisnaputra, O., Sulaeiman, N., Ware, L., Shaw, W., de Moor, C., & Graeff, J. (1992). The use of diarrhoeal management counseling cards for community health volunteer training in Indonesia: The HealthCom Project. *Journal of Tropical Medicine and Hygiene, 95,* 301-308.

Elder, J., Schmid, T., Hovell, M., Molgaard, C., & Graeff, J. (1989). The global relevance of behavioral medicine: Health and child survival in the developing world. *Annals of Behavioral Medicine, 11*(1), 12-17.

Emery, S., Gilpin, E. A., Ake, C., Farkas, A. J., & Pierce, J. P. (2000). Characterizing and identifying "hard-core" smokers: Implications for further reducing smoking prevalence. *American Journal of Public Health, 90,* 387-394.

Emri, S., Bagci, T., Karakoca, Y., & Baris, E. (1998). Recognition of cigarette brand names and logos by primary schoolchildren in Ankara, Turkey. *Tobacco Control, 7,* 386-392.

Escohotado A. (1998). *Historia de las drogas.* Madrid: Alianza Editorial.

Escohotado A. (1998). *Historia de las drogas.* Madrid: Alianza Editorial.

Ewart, C. K. (1991). Social action theory for a public health psychology. *American Psychologist, 46*(9), 931-946.

Fairchild, A., & Oppenheimer, G. (1998). Public health nihilism vs pragmatism: History, politics and the control of tuberculosis. *American Journal of Public Health, 88*(7), 1105-1117.

Farmer, P. (1996). Social inequalities and emerging infectious diseases. *Emerging Infectious Diseases, 2*(4), 259-269.

Fathalla, M. F. (1990). The challenges of safe motherhood. In H. Wallace (Ed.), *Health care of women and children in developing countries* (pp. 219-228). New York: Free Press.

Fauci, A. S. (1999). The AIDS epidemic. *New England Journal of Medicine, 341*(14), 1046-1050.

Fincancioglu, N. (1982). Carrots and sticks. *People, 9,* 3-11.

Gardner, G., & Halweil, B. (2000, March 9). The world pays a heavy price for malnutrition. *International Herald Tribune,* p. 9.

Gleissberg, V. (1999). The threat of multidrug resistance: Is tuberculosis ever untreatable or uncontrollable? *Lancet, 353,* 998-999.

Gordon, A. (1988). Mixed strategies in health education and community participation: An evaluation of dengue control in the Dominican Republic. *Health Education Research, Theory and Practice, 4,* 399-419.

Graeff, J., Elder, J., & Booth, E. (1993). *Communications for health behavior change: A developing country perspective.* San Francisco: Jossey-Bass.

Grange, J., & Zumla, A. (1999). Paradox of the global emergency of tuberculosis. *Lancet, 353,* 996.

Gregson, S., Zhuwau, T., Anderson, R., & Chandiwana, S. (1997). Is there evidence for behavior change in response to AIDS in rural Zimbabwe? *Social Science and Medicine, 46*(3), 321-30.

Gubler, D. J. (1989). *Aedes aegypti* and *Aedes aegypti*-borne disease in the 1990s: Top down or bottom up. *American Journal of Tropical Medical Hygiene, 40*(6), 571-578.

Guerra F. (1972). Historia de la adicción. *Tribuna Médica, 16.*

Guthrie, G., Guthrie, H., Fernandez, T., & Estrera, N. (1982). Cultural influences and reinforcements strategies. *Behavior Therapy, 13,* 624-637.

Gwatkin, D. R., Guillot, M., & Heuveline, P. (1999). The burden of disease among the global poor. *Lancet, 354,* 586-589.

Hafstad, A., Aaro, L. E., Engeland, A., Anderson, A., Langmark, F., & Stray-Pedersen, B. (1997). Provocative appeals in anti-smoking mass media campaigns in adolescents—the accumulated effect of multiple exposures. *Health Education Research, 12,* 227-236.

Harpham, T. (1993). Urbanisation in the third world: Health policy implications. In L. M. Schell, M. T. Smith, & A. Bilsborough (Eds.), *Urban ecology and health in the third world* (pp. 274-282). Cambridge, UK: Cambridge University Press.

Hinman, A. (1999). Eradication of vaccine-preventable diseases. *Annual Review of Public Health, 20,* 211-229.

Hoodfar, H., & Assadpour, S. (2000). The politics of population policy in the Islamic Republic of Iran. *Studies in Family Planning, 31*(1), 19-34.

Howard, C. R., & Weitzman, M. (1992). Breast or bottle: Practical aspects of infant nutrition in the first six months. *Pediatric Annuals, 10,* 619-631.

Hurst R. D. (1999). Tratar el tabaquismo e invertir la tendencia. *Boletin OMS, 1,* 8.

Hyde, L. (1999). HIV and drug users in Ukraine: Building confidence to reduce HIV risk. *Impact on HIV, 1*(2), 2-7.

Jacobsen, J. (1983). Promoting population stabilization: Incentives for small families. *Worldwatch Paper,* No. 54.

Jelliffe, D. B., & Jelliffe, E. F. P. (1990). *Growth monitoring and promotion in young children: Guidelines for the selection for the methods of training techniques.* New York: Oxford University Press.

Joesoeff, R., Annest, J., & Utomo, B. (1989). A recent increase of breastfeeding duration in Jakarta, Indonesia. *American Journal of Public Health, 79,* 36.

Joossens, L. (2000, April 1). *Impuestos, precio y contabando: Experiencies en diversos paises eurpeos.* Paper presented at the conference, Precio, impuestos, y contrabando de tabaco en España: Evolucion y relevancia para la salud, Madrid, Spain.

Kane, T., Gueye, M., Speizer, I., Pacque-Margolis, S., & Baron, D. (1998). The impact of a family planning multimedia campaign in Bamako, Mali. *Studies in Family Planning, 29*(3), 309-323.

Kanfer, F. H. (1975). Self-management methods. In F. Kanfer & A. Goldstein (Eds.), *Helping people change* (pp. 309-356). New York: Pergamon.

Kenya, P. R., Gatiti, S., Muthami, L. N., Agwanda, R., Mwenesi, H. A., Katsivo, M. N., Omondi-Odhiambo, Surrow, A., Juma, R., Ellison, R.H., Cooper, G., & van Andel, F. G. (1990). Oral rehydration therapy and social marketing in rural Kenya. *Social Science and Medicine, 31*(9), 979-987.

Kim-Farley, R. (1992). Global immunization. *Annual Review of Public Health, 13,* 223-237.

King, M. (1991). Malaria control and the demographic trap. *Lancet, 338*(8759), 124.

King, R., Estey, J., Allen, S., Kegeles, S., Wolf, W., Valentine, C., & Serufilira, A. (1995). A family planning intervention to reduce vertical transmission of HIV in Rwanda. *AIDS, 9*(Suppl. 1), 45-51.

Kosters, M. (1994). How poverty looks. *American Enterprise, 5*(5), 26-28.

Kotler, P., & Andreasen, A. (1996). *Strategic marketing for non-profit organizations* (2nd. ed.). Upper Saddle River, NJ: Prentice Hall.

Kotler, P., & Roberto, E. L. (1989). *Social marketing: Strategies for changing public behavior.* New York: Free Press.

Krauthammer, C. (1999, December 13). Return of the Luddites. *Time,* p. 25.

Kwon, K. H. (1971). Use of the agent system in Seoul. *Studies in Family Planning, 13,* 159-172.

Lalonde, M. (1974). *A new perspective on the health of Canadians.* Ottawa: Government of Canada.

Lappe, F. (1982). *Diet for a small planet.* New York: Ballantyne.

Lederberg, J., Shope, R. E., & Oaks, S. C. (1992). *Emerging infections: Microbial threats to health in the United States.* Washington, DC: National Academy Press.

Lewitt, E. M., Coate, D., & Grossman, M. (1981). The effects of government regulation on teenage smoking. *Journal of Law Economics, 24*(3), 545-569.

Linsk, J. A. (1993). American medical culture and the health care crisis. *American Journal of Medical Quality, 8*(4), 174-180.

Lloyd, L. (1991). *A community based Aedes aegypti control program in Merida, Yúcatan, Mexico.* Unpublished doctoral dissertation, the John Hopkins University, Baltimore, MD.

Lurie, P., Fernandes, M., Hughes, V., Arevalo, E., & Hudes, E. (1995). Socioeconomic status and risk of HIV-1: Syphilis and hepatitis B infection among sex workers in Sao Paulo State, Brazil. *AIDS, 9*(Suppl.), 31-37.

Lutter, C. K., Perez-Escamilla, R., Segall, A., Sanghvi, T., Teruya, K., & Wickham, C. (1997). The effectiveness of a hospital-based program to promote exclusive breast-feeding among low-income women in Brazil. *American Journal of Public Health, 87*(4), 659-663.

MacKay, J., & Crofton, J. (1996). Tobacco and the developing world. *British Medical Bulletin, 52*(1), 206-221.

Maher, D., Van Gorkom, J. L. C., Gondrie, P. C. F. M., & Raviglione, M. (1999). Community contribution to tuberculosis care in countries with high tuberculosis prevalence: Past, present, and future. *International Journal of Tuberculosis and Lung Disease, 3*(9), 762-768.

Masland, T., & Nordland, R. (2000, January 17). 10 million orphans. *Newsweek,* pp. 42-45.

Matulessy, P. (1988). The Indonesian national breastfeeding programme. In I. D. Jelliffe & P. Jelliffe (Eds), *Programmes to promote breastfeeding* (pp. 166-169). Oxford, UK: Oxford University Press.

McCann, T. V., & Sharkey, R. J. (1998). Educational intervention with international nurses and changes in knowledge, attitudes, and willingness to provide care to patients with HIV/AIDS. *Journal of Advanced Nursing, 27*(2), 267-273.

McGuire, T. (1981). Theoretical foundations of public communication campaigns. In R. Rice & W. Paisley (Eds.), *Public communication campaigns* (pp. 41-70). Beverly Hills, CA: Sage.

McKee, M., Bobak, M., Rose, R., Shkolnikov, V., Chenet, L., & Leon, D. (1998). Patterns of smoking in Russia. *Tobacco Control, 7,* 22-26.

McKeown, T., Record, R. G., & Turner, R. D. (1975). An interpretation of the decline of mortality in England and Wales during the 20th century. *Population Studies, 29,* 391-422.

McKinlay, J. B., & Marceau, L. D. (1999). A tale of 3 tails. *American Journal of Public Health, 89*(3), 295-298.

McKinlay, J. B., & Marceau, L. D. (2000). To boldly go. *American Journal of Public Health, 90*(1), 25-33.

Menzies, D., Tannenbaum, T. N., & FitzGerald, J. M. (1999). Tuberculosis: Prevention. *Canadian Medical Association Journal, 161*(6), 717-724.

Meremikwu, M. M., Asindi, A. A., & Antia-Obong, O. E. (1997). The influence of breast-feeding on the occurrence of dysentery, persistent diarrhoea, and malnutrition among Nigerian children with diarrhoea. *West African Journal of Medicine, 16*(1), 20-23.

Miller, K., & Rosenfield, A. (1996). Population and women's reproductive health: An international perspective. *Annual Review of Public Health, 17,* 359-382.

Montgomery, D. L., & Splett, P. L. (1997). Economic benefit of breast-feeding infants enrolled in WIC. *Journal of the American Dietetic Association, 97,* 379-385.

Morabia, A. (2000). Worldwide surveillance of risk factors to promote global health. *American Journal of Public Health, 90*(1), 22-24.

Morales, C. (1999). *Nicaragua: Filtro casero para el tratamiento de agua de consumo en el sector rural.* Unpublished document, Pan American Health Organization. Available: www.ops.org.ni

Morely, D. C. (1968). Health and weight chart for use in developing countries. *Tropical Geographical Medicine, 20,* 101.

Mueller, O., Cham, K., Jaffar, S., & Greenwood, B. (1997). The Gambian National Impregnated Bednet Programme: Evaluation of the 1994 cost recovery trial. *Social Science and Medicine, 44*(12), 1903-1909.

Mullan, F. (2000). Don Quixote, Machiavelli, and Robin Hood: Public health practice, past and present. *American Journal of Public Health, 90,* 702-706.

Murray, C. J. L., & Lopez, A. S. (1996, November). Evidence-based health policy—Lessons from the Global Burden of Disease Study. *Science, 274,* 740-743.

Murray, C. J. L., & Lopez, A. S. (1997a). Global mortality, disability, and the contribution of risk factors: Global Burden of Disease Study. *Lancet, 349,* 1498-1504.

Murray, C. J. L., & Lopez, A. S. (1997b). Mortality by cause for eight regions of the world: Global Burden of Disease study. *Lancet, 349,* 1269-1276.

Murray, C. J. L., & Salomon, J. A. (1998a). Expanding the WHO tuberculosis control strategy: Rethinking the role of active case-finding. *International Journal of Tuberculosis and Lung Disease, 2*(Suppl. 9), 15.

Murray, C. J. L., & Salomon, J. A. (1998b). Modeling the impact of global tuberculosis control strategies. *Proceedings of the National Academy of Sciences, 95,* 13881-13886.

Mustaque, A., Chowdhury, R., & Cash, R. (1996). *A simple solution: Teaching millions to treat diarrhoea at home.* Dhaka, Bangladesh: University Press Limited.

Muwango-Bayego, H. (1994). Tobacco growing in Uganda: The environment and women pay the price. *Tobacco Control, 3,* 255-256.

Myers, P. (1992). Reducing transportation fuel consumption: How far should we go? *Automotive Engineering, 100*(9), 89-95.

Myers, M. (1997). Consumption: Challenge to development. *Science, 276*(4), 53-55.

Negerá, J. A., Liese, B. H., & Hammer, J. (1993). Malaria. In D. T. Jamison, W. H. Mosley, A. R. Measham, & J. L. Bobadilla (Eds.), *Disease control priorities in developing countries* (pp. 281-302). London: Oxford Medical Publications.

Newton, N. (2000). *Applying best practices to youth reproductive health.* Arlington, VA: SEATS Project/John Snow.

The non-governmental order: Will NGOs democratize, or merely disrupt, global governance? (1999, December 11-17). *Economist,* pp. 18-19.

Obiora, L. A. (1999). Symbolic episodes in the quest for environmental justice. *Human Rights Quarterly, 21*(2), 464-512.

Pan American Health Organization/World Health Organization. (1986). *Guide for planning, implementing, and evaluating programs to control acute respiratory infections as part of primary health care* (Publication WHO/RSD 186.29). Washington, DC: Author.

Parlato, M., & Gottert, P. (1998). Lessons learned. In M. Parlato & R. Seidel (Eds.), *Large-scale application of nutrition behavior change approaches: Lessons from West Africa* (pp. 35-42). Arlington, VA: BASICS Project.

Parlato, M., & Seidel, R. (1998). *Application of nutrition behavior change approaches: Lessons from West Africa.* Arlington, VA: BASICS Project.

Perry, H., Robison, N., Chavez, D., Taja, O., Hilari, C., Shanklin, D., & Wyon, J. (1999). Attaining health for all through community partnerships: Principles of the census-based approach to primary health care developed in Bolivia, South America. *Social Science and Medicine, 48,* 1053-1067.

Peto, R., Lopez, A. D., Boreham, J., Thun, M., Heath, C., & Doll, R. (1996). Mortality from smoking worldwide. *British Medical Bulletin, 52*(1), 12-21.

Pillsbury, B. (1990). *Immunization: The behavioral issues.* Washington, DC: USAID Office of Health/International Health and Development.

Porter, J., & McAdam, K. (1994). The re-emergence of tuberculosis. *Annual Review of Public Health, 15,* 303-323.

Potts, M. (1997). Too many people pose global risk. *Forum for Applied Research and Public Policy, 12*(2), 6-15.

Prochaska, J. O., & DiClemente, C. C. (1983). Stages and processes of self-change in smoking: Towards an integrative model of change. *Journal of Consulting and Clinical Psychology, 51,* 390-395.

Prochaska, J. O., & DiClemente, C. C. (1998). Towards a comprehensive, transtheoretical model of change: Stages of change and addictive behaviors. In W. R. Miller & N. Heather (Eds.), *Treating addictive behaviors* (2nd ed.) (pp. 3-24). New York: Plenum.

Reid, D. (1996). Tobacco control: Overview. *British Medical Bulletin, 52*(1), 108-120.

Reid, T. (1998). Feeding the planet. *National Geographic, 4,* 56-75.

Reis, T., Elder, J., Satoto, Kodyat, B., & Palmer, A. (1991). An examination of the performance and motivation of Indonesian village health volunteers. *International Quarterly of Community Health Education, 11,* 19-27.

Reiter, P., & Gubler, D. J. (1997). Surveillance and control of urban dengue vectors. In D. Gubler & G. Kuno (Eds.), *Dengue and dengue hemorrhagic fever* (pp. 452-462). London: CAB International.

Rice, M., & Rasmusson, E. (1991). Healthy cities in developing countries. In J. Ashton (Ed), *Healthy cities* (pp. 70-84). Buckingham, UK: Open University Press.

Rivas, L., & Lloyd, L. (1996, August 22-24). *Recent advances in community-based control of aedes aegypti: Mexico.* Proceedings of a workshop held in Mérida, Yúcatan, Mexico. New York: The Rockefeller Foundation.

Robbins, J. (1987). *Diet for a new America.* Walpole, NH: Stillpoint.

Rogers, E. M. (1973). Incentives in the diffusion of family planning innovations. In E. Rogers (Ed.), *Communication strategies for family planning* (pp. 152-224). New York: Free Press.

Rogers, E. M. (1983). *Diffusion of innovations.* New York: Free Press.

Rogers, E., Vaughan, P., Swalehe, R., Rao, N., Svenderud, P., & Sood, S. (1999). Effects of an entertainment-education radio soap opera on family planning behavior in Tanzania. *Studies in Family Planning, 30*(3), 193-211.

Rose, G. (1992). *The strategy of preventive medicine.* Oxford, UK: Oxford University Press.

Rosen, G. (1993). *A history of public health* (expanded ed.). Baltimore, MD: The Johns Hopkins University Press.

Sagoff, M. (1997, June). Do we consume too much? *Atlantic,* pp. 80-96.

Samet, J. M., Yach, D., Taylor, C. E., Becker, K. M. (1998). Research for effective global tobacco control in the 21st century: Report of a working group convened during the 10th world conference on tobacco or health. *Tobacco Control, 7,* 72-77.

Satcher, D. (1995). Emerging infections: Getting ahead of the curve. *Emerging Infectious Diseases, 1*(1), 1-6.

Sharma, U. K., & Willingham, F. F. (1997). Breast-feeding and human immune deficiencies virus. *Indian Journal Pediatrics, 16,* 547-553.

Sherman, C., Fernandez, E. A., Chan, A. S., Lozano, R. C., Leontsini, E., & Winch, P. J. (1998). La untadita: A procedure for maintaining wash basins and drums free of *Aedes aegypti* based on modification of existing practices. *American Journal of Tropical Hygiene, 58*(2), 257-262.

Short, S., & Fengying, Z. (1998). Looking locally at China's one-child policy. *Studies in Family Planning, 29*(4), 373-87.

Siegel, M., Biener, L. (2000). The impact of antismoking media campaign on progression to established smoking: Results of a longitudinal youth study. *American Journal of Public Health, 90,* 380-386.

Sikkema, K., Kelly, J., Winett, R., Solomon, L., Cargill, V., Roffman, R., McAuliffe, T., Heckman, T., Anderson, E., Wagstaff, D., Norman, A., Perry M., Crumble, D., & Mercer, M. (2000). Outcomes of a randomized community-level HIV prevention intervention for women living in 18 low-income developments. *American Journal of Public Health, 90*(1), 57-63.

Simmons, R., Hall, P., Diaz, J., Diaz, M., Fajans, P., & Satia, J. (1997). The strategic approach to contraceptive introduction. *Studies in Family Planning, 28*(2), 79-94.

Singer, M. (1999, August 2). The population surprise. *Atlantic Monthly, 284,* 22-25.

Singh, K., Viegas, O., & Ratnam, S. (1985). Incentives and disincentives used to affect demographic changes in fertility trends in Singapore. *Singapore Medical Journal, 25,* 101-107.

Skinner, B. F. (1953). *Science and human behavior.* New York: Macmillan.

Soderlund, N., Lavis, J., Broomberg, J., & Mills, A. (1993). The costs of HIV prevention strategies in developing countries. *Bulletin of the World Health Organization, 71*(5), 595-604.

Soderlund, N., Zwi, K., Kinghorn, A., & Gray, G. (1999). Prevention of vertical transmission of HIV: Analysis of cost effectiveness of options available in South Africa. *British Medical Journal, 318,* 1650-1656.

Srison, D., Thisyakorn, U., Paupunwatana, S., Chotpitayasunondh, T., Kanchanamayul, V., Limpitikul, W., & Panpitpat, C. (1995). Perinatal HIV infections in Thailand. *Southeast Asian Journal of Tropical Medicine and Public Health, 26*(4), 659-663.

Stansfield, S. I., & Shepard, D. S. (1993). Acute respiratory infection. In D. T. Jamison, W. H. Mosley, A. R. Measham, & J. L. Bobadilla (Eds.), *Disease control priorities in developing countries* (pp. 67-90). London: Oxford Medical Publications.

Stuart-Harris, C., Western, K., & Chamberlayne, E. (1982). Can infectious diseases be eradicated? A report on the international conference on the eradication of infectious diseases. *Review of Infectious Diseases, 4,* 913-984.

Sulzer-Azaroff, B., & Mayer, G. R. (1991). *Behavior analysis for lasting change.* Fort Worth, TX: Harcourt Brace.

Tan, S. B., Lee, J., & Ratnam, S. (1978). Effects of social disincentive policies on fertility behavior in Singapore. *American Journal of Public Health, 68,* 119-125.

UNAIDS/WHO. (1999). Global AIDS statistics. *AIDS CARE, 11*(2), 253-264.

United Nations International Children's Education Fund (UNICEF). (1991). *Facts for life.* New York: Author.

U.S. Department of Health and Human Services. (1989). *Making health communications work—A planner's guide* (NIH Publication No. 89-1493). Washington, DC: Government Printing Office.

U.S. Department of Health and Human Services. (1998). *Healthy people in healthy communities.* Washington, DC: Government Printing Office.

Valente, T., Watkins, S., Jato, M., van der Straten, A., & Tsitsol, L.-P. (1997). Social network associations with contraceptive use among Cameroonian women in voluntary associations. *Social Science and Medicine, 45*(5), 677-687.

Vateesatokit, P., Hughes, B., & Ritthphakdee, B. (2000). Thailand: Winning battles, but the war's far from over. *Tobacco Control, 9,* 122-127.

Veatch, R. (1977). Governmental population incentives: Ethical issues at stake. *Studies in Family Planning, 8,* 100-108.

Venier, J., Ross, M., & Akande, A. (1997). HIV/AIDS-related social anxieties in adolescents in three African countries. *Social Science and Medicine, 46*(3), 313-320.

Victora, C., Morris, S., Barros, F., Horta, B., Weiderpass, E., & Tomasi, E. (1998). Breast-feeding and growth in Brazilian infants. *American Journal of Clinical Nutrition, 67,* 452-458.

Visness, C., & Kennedy, K., (1997). Maternal employment and breast-feeding: Findings from the 1988 National Maternal and Infant Health Survey. *American Journal of Public Health, 87*(6), 945-950.

Visrutaratna, S., Lindan, C. P., Sirhorachai, A., & Mandel, J. S. (1995). "Superstar" and "model brothel:" Developing and evaluating a condom promotion program for sex establishments in Chiang Mai, Thailand. *AIDS, 9*(Suppl. 1), 69-75.

Wald, N., & Hackshaw, A. K. (1996). Cigarette smoking: An epidemiological overview. *British Medical Bulletin, 52*(1), 3-11.

Wallace, H. (Ed.). (1990). *Health care for women and children in developing countries.* Oakland, CA: Third Party.

Wallace, C., & Elder, J. (1980). Statistics to evaluate measurement accuracy and treatment effects in single-subject research designs. In M. Hersen, R. Eisler, & P. Miller (Eds.), *Progress in behavior modification* (Vol. 10, pp. 39-79). New York: Academic Press.

Wallack, L. (1990). Improving health promotion: Media advocacy and social marketing approaches. In C. Atkin & L. Wallack (Eds.), *Mass communication and public health* (pp. 147-163). Newbury Park, CA: Sage.

Wallack, L., & Dorfman, L. (1996). Media advocacy: A strategy for advancing policy and promoting health. *Health Education Quarterly, 23,* 293-317.

Waluye, J. (1994). Environmental impact of tobacco growing in Tabora/Urambo, Tanzania. *Tobacco Control, 3,* 252-254.

Watanabe, M. (1997). U.S. agencies focusing on urban remediation. *Scientist, 11*(9), 1-4.

White, A. (1998). Senegal: Now you see it, now you don't—PM's April fool's joke on Clinton. *Tobacco Control, 7,* 340.

Wilkinson, D., Gcabashe, L., & Lurie, M. (1999). Traditional healers as tuberculosis treatment super-visors: Precedent and potential. *International Journal of Tuberculosis and Lung Disease, 3*(9), 833-842.

Wilmoth, T., & Elder, J. (1995). An assessment of research on breastfeeding promotion strategies in developing countries. *Social Science and Medicine,* 1-16.

Worden, J. K., Flynn, B. S., Solomon, L. J., Secker-Walker, R. H., Badger, G. J., & Carpenter, J. H. (1996). Using mass media to prevent cigarette smoking among adolescent girls. *Health Education Quarterly, 23,* 453-468.

World Bank. (1997). *Health, nutrition, and population.* Washington, DC: Author.

World Health Organization. (1978). *Report on the international conference on primary health care, USSR, September 6-12, 1978.* Geneva, Switzerland: Author.

Young, J. E., & Sachs, A. (1995). Creating a sustainable materials economy. In L. Brown, C. Flavin, & H. French (Eds), *State of the world* (pp. 76-94), New York: Norton.

Zierler, S., & Krieger, N. (1997). Reframing women's risk: Social inequalities and HIV infection. *Annual Review of Public Health, 18,* 401-436.

Name Index

Subject Index

About the Author

John P. Elder is currently Professor of Public Health at San Diego State University and adjunct professor of pediatrics at the University of California—San Diego. He holds the PhD in psychology from West Virginia University and the MPH from Boston University. Prior to coming to San Diego, he was on the community medicine faculty at Brown University. Guest faculty appointments include the National School of Public Health in Spain and the Magdeburg (Germany) Polytechnic Institute. Dr. Elder has written three books and nearly 200 articles and chapters. He has worked on child survival, vector control, environmental protection, and chronic disease prevention projects in 20 countries in the Americas, the Middle East, Europe, Asia, and the Southwest Pacific.